STARK

# KOMPAKT-WISSEN
# REALSCHULE

Rainer Jacob

# Englisch – Themenwortschatz

STARK

ISBN 978-3-89449-855-9


D-85318 Freising · Postfach 1852 · Tel. (08161)1790
Auflage 2008

# Inhalt

# Vorwort

Liebe Schülerin, lieber Schüler,

du hast sicher schon gemerkt, wie wichtig Vokabeln im Englischunterricht sind. Egal ob es darum geht, einen Text richtig zu verstehen, Fragen zu beantworten, einen Brief oder sonstigen Text zu verfassen – immer brauchst du einen umfangreichen Wortschatz. Damit du sicher und gut gerüstet in Klassenarbeiten und in deine Realschulabschlussprüfung gehen kannst, bietet dir dieser Band doppelte Hilfe an.

- Zum einen sind die Vokabeln zu den wichtigsten Themen, die im Unterricht behandelt werden, übersichtlich in einzelnen Kapiteln zusammengestellt. Auf diese Weise lassen sie sich leichter lernen. Außer der deutschen Bedeutung des Wortes findest du auch einen Beispielsatz: Erst durch die Verwendung des Wortes in einem sinnvollen Zusammenhang wird dir klar, wie du das Wort anwenden kannst. Hier kannst du auch Synonyme und Antonyme nachsehen.

- Zum anderen enthält unser Themenwortschatz einen umfangreichen Nachschlageteil mit dem Grundwortschatz für die Realschule. Dort kannst du alle Wörter, die du (noch) nicht kennst, nachschlagen, um sie dann zu lernen und in deinen Wortschatz aufzunehmen.

Viel Erfolg für deine Klassenarbeiten und die Realschulabschlussprüfung!

Rainer Jacob

# Abkürzungsverzeichnis

| | |
|---|---|
| AE | American English |
| BE | British English |
| a.m. | vormittags |
| p.m. | nachmittags |
| jmdm. | jemandem |
| jmdn. | jemanden |
| Pl. | Plural |
| s.o. | someone |
| sth. | something |
| = | Synonym |
| ≠ | Antonym |
| [ɪ] | Lautschrift, die erklärt, wie ein Wort ausgesprochen wird |

# Around the World

| vocabulary | dt. Bedeutung | English sentence | syn/opp |
|---|---|---|---|
| abroad | *im Ausland, aus dem Ausland* | Fishing in Ireland attracts many tourists from abroad. | = overseas |
| (to) afford | *sich etwas leisten* | My parents will lend me the money, otherwise I couldn't afford the trip to Cambridge. | |
| amazing<br>(to) amaze<br>amazement | *erstaunlich*<br>*erstaunen*<br>*Erstaunen* | New Zealand has an amazing wildlife ("Tier- und Pflanzenwelt"). | = astonishing |
| apartment | *Wohnung* | We spent five days in the London apartment of my friend Gerry. | |
| (to) apply<br>application | *beantragen, sich bewerben*<br>*Bewerbung* | If you need a visa, you should apply early. | |
| arrival<br>(to) arrive | *Ankunft*<br>*ankommen* | On our arrival we were greeted by our guest parents. | ≠ departure |
| (to) attempt<br>attempt | *versuchen*<br>*Versuch* | An American scientific team attempted to find the monster in Loch Ness. | = (to) try hard, (to) make an effort |
| (to) attract<br>attractive | *anziehen*<br>*attraktiv, anziehend* | Today many tourists are attracted by the wax figures in Madame Tussauds. | |
| (to) avoid | *vermeiden* | It is good to get to the air-port in time in order to avoid problems. | |
| bed and breakfast | *Übernachtung mit Frühstück* | In England you can find a lot of places which offer bed and breakfast. | |

| vocabulary | dt. Bedeutung | English sentence | syn/opp |
| --- | --- | --- | --- |
| (to) board | *an Bord gehen, einsteigen* | We still have two hours left before we have to board our plane. | |
| boarding house | *Pension* | We stayed at a boarding house at the beach. | |
| (to) book | *buchen* | I book my holiday at the last minute. | |
| booking | *Reservierung, Buchung* | The hotel manager is happy about the number of bookings during the summer months. | |
| (to) borrow | *sich etwas (aus-) leihen, etwas ent-leihen* | American country music borrowed elements from European folk music as well as from the Negro blues. | |
| busy | *belebt* | Oxford Street is extremely busy at Christmas shopping time. | |
| (to) camp<br>camping<br>camp(ing) site, camping ground [AE] | *zelten, lagern*<br>*Camping, Zelten*<br>*Campingplatz* | Sonia and her friends went camping.<br>The camp sites in Cornwall were full of tourists. | |
| camping van | *Wohnmobil* | Mr and Mrs Taylor have bought a camping van. | |
| capital | *Hauptstadt* | The capital of the USA is Washington, D.C. | |
| (to) cash | *einlösen* | I cashed a 100-dollar-cheque at the Bank of America. | |
| (to) check in | *sich anmelden* | We checked in at our hotel in the afternoon. | ≠ (to) check out |
| climate | *Klima* | People from the Continent are often not happy about Britain's climate. | |

| vocabulary | dt. Bedeutung | English sentence | syn/opp |
|---|---|---|---|
| coast | *Küste* | From coast to coast the USA is about 2,800 miles wide. | |
| comfortable<br>comfort | *bequem*<br>*Bequemlichkeit* | Our seats on the plane were very comfortable. | |
| (to) comment | *sich zu etwas äußern, einen Kommentar abgeben* | People in Britain always comment on the weather. | |
| commercial | *Handels-, kaufmännisch, wirtschaftlich* | The City is the commercial centre of London where the international banks are. | |
| commerce | *Handel* | | |
| convenient | *praktisch, bequem* | For most older people staying at a hotel is more convenient than camping. | |
| countryside | *Landschaft* | We toured Wales and enjoyed its beautiful countryside. | |
| credit card | *Kreditkarte* | In the USA credit cards are accepted in almost all shops and restaurants. | |
| crowded | *(mit Menschen) überfüllt* | Between 7 and 9 in the morning underground trains are crowded. | |
| (to) decide<br>decision | *sich entscheiden*<br>*Entscheidung* | Last summer we decided to stay at home during our holidays. | |
| (to) delay | *(sich) verspäten, verzögern* | Our flight to Majorca was three hours delayed because of engine problems. | |
| departure<br>(to) depart | *Abreise, Abfahrt*<br>*abfahren, abreisem* | Departure of the train to Glasgow will be at ten past three. | |

| vocabulary | dt. Bedeutung | English sentence | syn/opp |
|---|---|---|---|
| (to) depend | *abhängen (abhängig sein von)* | Many US states – including Florida, Hawaii, and Colorado – depend on tourism. | |
| desert | *Wüste* | Some southern parts of the Rocky Mountains are dry like deserts. | |
| destination | *Reiseziel* | Jackson Hole in the USA is a popular skiing destination. | |
| (to) destroy<br>destruction | *zerstören, vernichten*<br>*Zerstörung* | Hurricane Katrina destroyed beautiful wooden houses in New Orleans. | |
| distant<br>distance | *fern*<br>*Entfernung* | In Britain the sea never seems very distant, however far inland one is. It's only 71 miles to the sea. | = far away |
| (to) draw | *anziehen, ziehen* | Disney World Florida draws millions of visitors each year. | |
| (to) earn | *Geld verdienen* | New Zealand earns a lot of money from tourism. | |
| earthquake | *Erdbeben* | Experts fear that the next earthquake could kill thousands of people in San Francisco. | |
| enjoyable<br>(to) enjoy<br>enjoyment | *angenehm*<br>*genießen*<br>*Freude, Vergnügen* | Our stay in Inverness was very enjoyable. | |
| entrance<br>(to) enter | *Zugang, Eingang*<br>*betreten, eintreten* | The entrance from the Pacific Ocean through Golden Gate into San Francisco Bay is very small. | |
| exchange visit | *Schüleraustausch* | Next year I will take part in an exchange visit to Australia. | |

| vocabulary | dt. Bedeutung | English sentence | syn/opp |
|---|---|---|---|
| excited<br>exciting<br>excitement | *aufgeregt*<br>*aufregend*<br>*Aufregung* | The day before my first flight I was so excited I couldn't sleep half the night. | |
| excursion | *Ausflug, Exkursion* | Our excursion to the island of Malta was organized by Orion Tours International. | |
| (to) experience<br>experience | *erleben*<br>*Erlebnis, Erfahrung* | Seeing Manhattan is a wonderful experience. | |
| famous<br>fame | *berühmt*<br>*Ruhm* | Many famous museums are still free to students. | |
| flight<br>(to) fly | *Flug*<br>*fliegen* | During our flight to New York we ate two meals and we watched a film. | |
| gift shop | *Geschenkartikelladen* | We stopped at the gift shop to buy some souvenirs. | |
| guide<br>(to) guide | *Reiseführer*<br>*führen, leiten* | On our tour of Hadrian's Wall our guide told us everything about the Romans in Britain. | |
| guidebook | *Reiseführer* | A list of hotels can be found in the tourist guide book. | |
| (to) hire | *mieten* | My father hired a boat for a week on the Norfolk Broads last summer. | = (to) rent |
| holiday job | *Ferienarbeit* | Zoe took a holiday job in a restaurant. | |
| holiday maker | *Urlauber* | Most holiday makers like the food which they get at their hotels. | |
| holiday resort | *Ferienort* | Bournemouth is a popular holiday resort on the south coast of England. | |

| vocabulary | dt. Bedeutung | English sentence | syn/opp |
|---|---|---|---|
| host | *Gastgeber* | We wrote a thank-you-letter to our hosts, the Brandon family. | ≠ guest |
| host family | *Gastfamilie* | Simone was very happy in her American host family. | |
| (to) inhabit | *bewohnen* | The people of Trinidad inhabit one of the most beautiful islands in the Caribbean ("Karibik"). | |
| (to) invent<br>invention | *erfinden*<br>*Erfindung* | Bungee-jumping was invented in New Zealand. | |
| journey | *Reise* | Because of a strike in Calais we could not continue our journey to England. | = trip |
| lake | *See* | Loch Ness is a lake in Scotland which may be the home of a "monster". | |
| landmark | *Wahrzeichen* | Big Ben is one of London's most famous landmarks. | = sight |
| lost property office | *Fundbüro* | The lost property office is open 24 hours. | |
| means of transport | *Transportmittel, Beförderungsmittel* | Aeroplanes are still the safest means of transport. | |
| (to) mind<br>I don't mind | *ausmachen*<br>*es macht mir nichts aus* | I didn't mind walking around in the rain. | |
| (to) miss | *etwas verpassen* | Hardly any tourist who visits London misses a tour of the Tower to see the Crown Jewels. | |
| national park | *Nationalpark* | Yellowstone national park was opened in 1872. | |

| vocabulary | dt. Bedeutung | English sentence | syn/opp |
|---|---|---|---|
| native | *einheimisch* | Native Americans ("Indianer") have lived in the Grand Canyon region for many centuries. | |
| original<br>origin | *ursprünglich*<br>*Ursprung, Herkunft* | The bridges in London across the river Thames were originally wooden bridges. | |
| overseas | *Auslands-, ausländisch* | Overseas visitors are often surprised about American lifestyles. | |
| package holiday<br>package tour | *Pauschalurlaub*<br>*Pauschalreise* | The first foreign package holiday was a tour of Germany organised by Thomas Cook in 1855. | |
| particularly | *besonders, vor allem* | Tourism is a particularly important part of the economy. | = especially |
| passenger | *Passagier, Fluggast* | The passengers of flight LH4740 were called to gate 62. | |
| passport | *Reisepass* | When you travel in Europe you normally do not need a passport. | |
| peaceful<br>peace | *friedlich*<br>*Friede* | We enjoyed the peaceful beaches around the coast. | |
| popular<br>popularity | *beliebt*<br>*Beliebtheit* | Rome is a popular city for tourists. | |
| population<br>(to) populate | *Bevölkerung*<br>*bevölkern* | San Francisco has the largest Chinese population of any city outside China. | |
| (to) protect<br>protection | *schützen*<br>*Schutz* | National parks help to protect animals and plants. | |

| vocabulary | dt. Bedeutung | English sentence | syn/opp |
|---|---|---|---|
| **public transport** | *öffentliche Verkehrmittel* | Public transport in London is very expensive. | |
| **reception**<br>**(to) receive** | *Empfang*<br>*erhalten, empfangen* | We paid our hotel bill at the reception (desk). | |
| **receptionist** | *Empfangschef, Empfangsdame (im Hotel)* | Mr Nash worked as a receptionist in Dubai, St Moritz and New York. | |
| **(to) rent** | *mieten, leihen* | In Los Angeles we rented a car to drive around California and Arizona. | = (to) hire |
| **(to) request**<br>**request** | *bitten*<br>*Bitte, Wunsch* | Passengers were requested not to smoke during the whole flight. | |
| **reservation**<br>**(to) reserve** | *Reservierung*<br>*reservieren* | We had made a reservation because we knew that the hotel would be ful in August. | |
| **resort** | *Urlaubsort, Ferienort* | Padstow is a beautiful resort by the sea in Cornwall. | |
| **route** | *Route, Strecke* | Our route took us along the south-west coast of England. | |
| **rush-hour** | *Hauptverkehrszeit* | If you want to go into the centre of London try not to travel during the rush-hour. | |
| **scenery** | *Landschaft* | America's Great West is famous for its beautiful scenery. | |
| **seaside resort** | *Seebad* | Many British families spend their holidays at seaside resorts such as Blackpool, Brighton or Torquay. | |

| vocabulary | dt. Bedeutung | English sentence | syn/opp |
|---|---|---|---|
| security | *Sicherheit, Sicherheitsvorkehrungen* | When you want to fly to the USA you have to go through several security checks at the airport. | |
| secure | *sicher* | | = safe |
| serious | *ernst, ernsthaft* | America's big cities have serious problems with traffic and crime. | |
| shopping trip | *Einkaufstour* | Alan and Rita are going on a shopping trip to France. | |
| (to) see | *sehen* | So far nobody has seen a monster in Loch Ness. | |
| sight | *Sehenswürdigkeit* | Golden Gate Bridge is one of the well-known sights of San Francisco. | = landmark |
| sightseeing | *Besichtigung(en)* | We did our sightseeing tour of Edinburgh on an open double-decker bus. | |
| (to) go sightseeing | *Besichtigungen machen* | | |
| single room | *Einzelzimmer* | I booked a single room. | |
| site | *Ort, Platz* | Niagara Falls is one of the most beautiful natural sites. | |
| (to) spend | *verbringen* | The Youngs always spend their summer holidays in the Canary Islands. | |
| (to) take off | *starten* | You should arrive at the airport two hours before your plane takes off. | |
| term | *Ausdruck* | The official term for the British isles is "The United Kingdom". | = name |
| tour | *Rundreise, Tour* | Harriet is planning a bike tour in the Lake District. | |
| tourism | *Tourismus* | A lot of San Francisco's money comes from banking and tourism. | |

| vocabulary | dt. Bedeutung | English sentence | syn/opp |
|---|---|---|---|
| tourist attraction | *Anziehungspunkt für Touristen* | The Empire State building is one of the many tourist attractions in New York. | |
| tourist information | *Fremdenverkehrsamt* | If you are looking for a place to stay it's best to ask at the tourist information. | = tourist office |
| tour operator | *Reiseveranstalter* | Some tour operators offer bungee jumping in Nepal. | |
| traveller<br>(to) travel | *Reisender*<br>*reisen* | Travellers can get to England by ferry ("Fähre") or through the Channel tunnel. | |
| travel agent | *Reisebürokaufmann, Reisebürokauffrau* | The travel agent worked out the prices for a caravan holiday in Ireland. | |
| travel agent's, travel agency | *Reisebüro* | I went to the travel agent's to pick up brochures about holidays in Wales. | |
| traveller's cheque | *Reisescheck* | In an American supermarket you can pay by traveller's cheques. | |
| valley | *Tal* | I would like to see the Valley of the Kings in Egypt ("Ägypten"). | |
| (to) vary | *variieren, wechseln, schwanken* | The climate in the Rocky Mountains varies a great deal. | |
| varied<br>variety | *vielfältig*<br>*Vielfalt* | | |
| youth hostel | *Jugendherberge* | The German schoolteacher Richard Schirrmann developed the idea of youth hostels around 1900. | |

# Family

| vocabulary | dt. Bedeutung | English sentence | syn/opp |
|---|---|---|---|
| (to) adopt | *adoptieren, die Patenschaft übernehmen (für)* | Thomas and Melanie Wells adopted a child from Peru. | |
| adoption | *Übernahme, Patenschaft* | | |
| adult | *Erwachsener* | In some US states children of 15 can drive a car if they are accompanied ("begleitet") by an adult. | = grown-up ≠ youngster, kid |
| ancestor | *Vorfahr(e)/ Vorfahrin* | Shail is British but his ancestors came from India. | ≠ descendant |
| aunt | *Tante* | Aunt Mary will lend me some money for a new computer. | |
| (to) bring up | *jmdn. aufziehen, erziehen* | Jim was brought up by his grandfather. | = (to) educate, (to) raise |
| birth | *Geburt* | | |
| birthday | *Geburtstag* | When is your birthday? | |
| care | *Sorge, Sorgfalt* | Caring for children is a fulltime job. | = (to) look after |
| (to) care for | *sich kümmern um* | | |
| (to) take care of | *sich um etwas kümmern, für etwas Sorge tragen* | An au pair girl has to take care of a home and a family. | |
| careful | *sorgfältig, vorsichtig* | | |
| childhood | *Kindheit* | Anne spent her childhood in New Zealand. | |
| couple | *(Ehe-) Paar* | The newly married couple went on honeymoon ("Hochzeitsreise") to Barbados. | |

| vocabulary | dt. Bedeutung | English sentence | syn/opp |
|---|---|---|---|
| cousin | *Cousin, Cousine* | I'd like you to meet my cousin Jennifer. | |
| date of birth | *Geburtsdatum* | Dwane's date of birth is January 3, 1996. | |
| descendant | *Nachkomme* | 100 descendants of Italian immigrants visited Ellis Island yesterday. | ≠ ancestor |
| divorce | *Scheidung* | Jane decided to get a divorce from Adam. | ≠ marriage |
| divorced | *geschieden* | Alan's parents are divorced. | ≠ married |
| familiar | *vertraut* | Then, suddenly, I heard a loud, familiar voice. | = well-known<br>≠ unfamiliar |
| female | *weiblich* | The number of female workers has increased recently. | ≠ male |
| foster child | *Pflegekind* | a child who is taken care of by a couple who are not his/her natural parents | |
| (to) give birth to a child | *ein Kind gebären* | Sarah gave birth to her second child at 29. | = (to) bear a child |
| grandchild | *Enkel, Enkelin* | Mr Reeves likes playing with his grandchildren. | |
| grandparents | *Großeltern* | When I can't get what I want from my mother, I always ask my grand-parents. | |
| grandson<br>granddaughter | *Enkel*<br>*Enkelin* | President John F. Kennedy was the grandson of Irish immigrants. | |
| household | *Haushalt* | Nearly all households have telephone and TV today. | |
| housework<br>(to) do house-work | *Hausarbeit*<br>*Hausarbeit machen* | After returning from the office Selma Pickwing has to do her housework. | |

| vocabulary | dt. Bedeutung | English sentence | syn/opp |
|---|---|---|---|
| human being | *Mensch* | All human beings should enjoy the same rights. | = man |
| husband | *Ehemann* | Mrs Miller's husband works as a mechanic. | ≠ wife |
| individual | *individuell, persönlich* | Everybody has his individual likes and dislikes. | ≠ general, common |
| kid | *Kind, Jugendliche(r)* | A new kid from Ireland moved into our neighbourhood. | = youngster ≠ adult, grown-up |
| marriage | *Heirat, Ehe* | My parents can look back on 20 years of marriage. | ≠ divorce |
| (to) marry | *heiraten* | She would only marry for love, not for money. | ≠ (to) divorce |
| member | *Mitglied (Familien-) Angehörige(r)* | At my grandfather's birthday all members of the family came together. | |
| membership | *Mitgliedschaft* | The membership in our football club is going down. | |
| neighbour | *Nachbar* | We often help our neighbours and they help us. | |
| neighbourhood | *Nachbarschaft, Viertel* | We live in a quiet neighbourhood. | |
| nephew | *Neffe* | Harry is the son of my elder sister Jane. He is my nephew. | |
| niece | *Nichte* | Carly is the daughter of my younger brother Tom. She is my niece. | |
| orphan | *Waise (-nkind)* | Oliver lost his parents as a baby and grew up as an orphan. | |
| place of birth | *Geburtsort* | | |
| pregnancy | *Schwangerschaft* | The increase in teenage pregnancies is disturbing ("beunruhigend"). | |

| vocabulary | dt. Bedeutung | English sentence | syn/opp |
|---|---|---|---|
| pregnant<br>(to) be ~<br>(to) get ~<br>(to) become ~ | *schwanger*<br>*~ sein*<br>*~ werden* | Mrs Miller is pregnant with her fourth child.<br><br>Muriel became pregnant when she was 17. | |
| (to) raise | *aufziehen, großziehen* | Mrs Muir raised her five children alone. | = (to) bring up |
| relative | *Verwandter* | a member of one's family | |
| (to) separate | *sich trennen* | After 15 years of marriage his parents separated. | |
| single | *ledig* | Women remain single longer today. | ≠ married |
| single mother | *allein erziehende Mutter* | Sophie is a single mother and works full time. | |
| single parent | *Alleinerziehende(r)* | a person who looks after their child or children without a husband or wife | |
| (to) start a family | *eine Familie gründen* | They started a family when they were still teenagers. | |
| (to) support a family | *eine Familie ernähren* | Jeremy, who is 16 and still goes to school, and cannot support a family. | |
| twin | *Zwilling* | The Carlyn twins look very much alike. | |
| wedding | *Hochzeit* | Next week I'll go to my sister's wedding. | |
| wife | *Ehefrau* | Harry and his wife explained to me how they cook for 60 people every day. | ≠ husband |
| youngster | *Jugendlicher* | Teachers complain that many youngsters cannot concentrate. | = teenager, kid |
| youth | *Jugendlicher; Jugend* | Black youths love watching basketball. | |

# School

| vocabulary | dt. Bedeutung | English sentence | syn/opp |
|---|---|---|---|
| assembly | *Versammlung* | In England school starts with assembly at 9 o'clock every morning. | |
| (to) assemble | *sich versammeln* | All school children assemble in the auditorium. | = (to) come together, (to) meet |
| assignment | *Aufgabe, Hausaufgabe* | Read all the assignments first before you start on your answers. | = task, exercise, homework |
| at school | *in der Schule* | Did you have a good day at school? | |
| (to) attend | *besuchen* | About 9 million pupils in the UK attend state schools. | = (to) go to school |
| basic skill | *Grundfertigkeit* | Reading, writing and arithmetic – the "three R's" – are basic skills. | |
| (to) be good at | *gut sein in* | Eric is very good at sport – he is our best footballer. | ≠ (to) be bad/weak at |
| boarding school | *Internat* | At the age of 8 Prince William was sent to a boarding school. | |
| bullying | *Tyrannisieren, Ärgern, Einschüchtern* | Bullying makes life at school very difficult for boys and girls. | |
| bullly | *Tyrann, gemeiner Mitschüler* | I remember Barry Oldham only too well – he was one of the worst bullies at my school. | |
| (to) bully | *ärgern, einschüchtern, mobben* | | = (to) annoy, (to) frighten, (to) intimidate |
| certificate | *Urkunde* | My certificate shows that I took exams in English, Maths and German. | |

| vocabulary | dt. Bedeutung | English sentence | syn/opp |
|---|---|---|---|
| charge<br>(to) be in charge of | *Verantwortung*<br>*verantwortlich sein für* | A headmaster is in charge of a school. | |
| (to) cheat | *schummeln, betrügen* | It never pays to cheat at school. | |
| chemistry | *Chemie* | My uncle is professor of chemistry at the University of Bristol. | |
| (to) choose<br>choice | *wählen*<br>*Auswahl* | In the USA pupils can choose some of their school subjects. | |
| classmate | *Klassenkamerad* | Simon always helps his classmates: He lets them copy his homework. | = schoolmate |
| composition | *Aufsatz* | I wrote a composition about my visit to Disney World in Orlando, Florida. | = essay |
| comprehensive school | *Gesamtschule* | Mary-Ann attends a big comprehensive school with over two thousand children. | |
| compulsory | *obligatorisch, verpflichtend* | Education in Britain is compulsory for all children between 5 and 16. | = obligatory<br>≠ voluntary |
| (to) copy | *abschreiben, kopieren* | Use your own words in your answers. Do not copy from the text. | |
| (to) correct<br>correction | *korrigieren*<br>*Korrektur* | Teachers say they spend more time correcting than teaching. | = (to) mark |
| curriculum | *Lehrplan* | Since 1989 England and Wales have a new national curriculum. | |

| vocabulary | dt. Bedeutung | English sentence | syn/opp |
|---|---|---|---|
| day out | *(Tages-) Ausflug* | Last Tuesday we had a day out at the zoo in Regent's Park. | = school trip, excursion |
| (to) do homework | *Hausaufgaben machen* | Simon always does his homework straight after school. | |
| domestic science | *Hauswirtschaftslehre, -kunde* | In domestic science students learn how to cook. | |
| (to) do well | *gut abschneiden* | Students work hard to do well in their exams. | |
| drama group | *Theatergruppe, Theatertruppe* | I am a member of our school drama group. | |
| (to) drop out of school | *die Schule abbrechen, vorzeitig verlassen* | Jake dropped out of school and started working at a supermarket. | |
| education | *Ausbildung, Bildung* | Parents want their children to have a good education. | |
| (to) educate | *erziehen, ausbilden* | | |
| educated | *gebildet* | You can soon tell if a person is educated or not. | |
| effect | *Wirkung, Auswirkung* | Pupils know that exams have a big effect on their future. | |
| (to) enter | *eintreten* | In 1995 Prince William entered the exclusive Eton College. | |
| | *teilnehmen an* | Jessica entered a beauty competition. | |
| entry | *Zugang* | | |
| entry test | *Aufnahmeprüfung, Zulassungstest* | The entry test to Ealing Arts College is very difficult. | |
| essay | *Aufsatz* | Jane had to write an essay on George Washington. | = composition |

| vocabulary | dt. Bedeutung | English sentence | syn/opp |
|---|---|---|---|
| exam | *Prüfung* | May, June and July are the main months for exams at English schools. | = test |
| exchange programme | *Austausch-programm* | Every year hundreds of young people from all over Europe take part in an exchange programme and spend a year in the United States. | |
| excursion | *Ausflug, Exkursion* | The class went on an excursion to Windsor Castle. | = school trip |
| (to) go on an excursion | *einen Ausflug machen* | | |
| exercise book | *Heft* | Open your exercise books, please. | |
| extra classes | *Nachhilfe* | Irene has extra classes in maths and physics. | |
| (to) fail | *nicht bestehen, durchfallen* | If an American student fails a number of subjects, he does not have to stay at high school for an extra year. | ≠ (to) pass |
| failure | *Versagen, Misserfolg* | | |
| (to) finish school | *die Schule beenden* | As soon as I finish school I want to work and earn some money. | ≠ (to) start school |
| foreign language | *Fremdsprache* | In our world foreign languages are becoming more and more important. | ≠ native language, mother tongue |
| form teacher | *Klassenlehrer* | Mr Finlay is our new form teacher – he is Scottish. | = form master, form mistress |

| vocabulary | dt. Bedeutung | English sentence | syn/opp |
|---|---|---|---|
| GCSE (= General Certificate of Secondary Education) | *Schulabschluss mit 16* | English pupils take their GCSE exams between May and July. | |
| graduate<br>(to) graduate | *Absolvent, Abgänger*<br>*die Abschlussprüfung bestehen, abgehen von* | University graduates have better chances of finding a good job. | |
| grammar school | *Gymnasium* | In England, grammar schools hardly exist today. Most children go to comprehensive schools. | |
| (to) hate<br>hate, hatred | *hassen*<br>*Hass* | I always liked school, but my sister hated it. | ≠ (to) love<br>≠ love, affection |
| headmaster | *Schulleiter, Direktor* | The new headmaster was strictly against kissing at school. | |
| headmistress | *Schulleiterin, Direktorin* | | |
| high school [AE] | *Oberstufenschule (14–18)* | After high school, Dwayne wants to go to Berkeley University in California. | |
| (to) improve<br>improvement | *sich verbessern, besser machen/werden*<br>*Verbesserung* | One of the best ways for a girl to improve her English is to work as an au pair. | |
| infant school [BE] | *Vorschule, Spielschule* | Children between 5 and 7 years of age go to infant schools. | = elementary school [AE] |
| (to) interrupt | *unterbrechen* | Noisy kids often interrupt the lessons. | |
| language course | *Sprachkurs* | In my holidays I want to attend a language course. | |

| vocabulary | dt. Bedeutung | English sentence | syn/opp |
|---|---|---|---|
| (to) leave | *verlassen* | Steve left school and worked in a fast food restaurant. | = (to) finish school<br>≠ (to) start school |
| lesson | *Unterrichtsstunde, Lektion* | Every Tuesday we have two English lessons. | |
| library | *Bücherei* | Jenny and Julie help organize our school library. | |
| (to) mark | *benoten, bewerten, korrigieren* | Our maths teacher says he has too many papers to mark. | |
| marks | *Noten* | Oliver is working hard to get better marks in English and French. | |
| maths | *Mathe (Kurzform)* | Hannah is not good at maths. | |
| meeting | *Versammlung, Besprechung, Treffen* | The meeting between parents and teachers began shortly after six. | |
| native language | *Muttersprache* | Many people in Florida speak Spanish as their native language. | = mother tongue<br>≠ foreign language |
| native speaker | *Muttersprachler* | The Chinese language has 1.1 billion native speakers. | |
| numeracy | *Rechnen* | For school children between 7 and 11 numeracy is one of the most important skills they learn. | |
| O-level (= Ordinary Level) | *Mittlere Reife* | Harriet took O-level exams in six subjects. | |
| oral | *mündlich* | I hate oral exams. I just get too nervous. | ≠ written |

| vocabulary | dt. Bedeutung | English sentence | syn/opp |
|---|---|---|---|
| (to) pass | *(eine Prüfung) bestehen* | All my classmates hope that we will pass our final exams next summer. | ≠ (to) fail |
| PE (= Physical Education) | *Sportunterricht* | Parents and teachers want children to have more physical education. | = sport |
| pen friend | *Brieffreund* | My French pen friend Michelle will come and visit me next summer. | |
| performance | *Leistung* | Ritchie trains hard every week, but he is not happy with his performance. | = achievement |
| performance | *Vorstellung, Aufführung* | The performances of our school drama group are always good. | = show |
| physics | *Physik* | Most pupils find physics too abstract. | |
| (to) praise | *loben* | The headmistress praised Tim and Christina for their work for the school magazine. | ≠ (to) tell s.o. off |
| (to) prepare | *sich vorbereiten* | Pupils learn and prepare for exams. | = (to) get ready |
| pressure | *Druck* | Exam pressure is a problem for many pupils. | = stress |
| (to) put pressure on | *Druck ausüben auf* | | |
| primary school | *Grundschule* | After primary school English kids go to a secondary school. | |
| public school [BE] | *Privatschule* | Eton, Harrow, Winchester, Westminster and Rugby are famous English public schools. | ≠ state school |

| vocabulary | dt. Bedeutung | English sentence | syn/opp |
|---|---|---|---|
| (to) punish | *(be)strafen* | It is necessary to punish hooligans hard. | ≠ (to) praise |
| punishment | *Strafe* | As a punishment football hooligans are not allowed to travel to away games. | |
| pupil | *Schüler* | The number of pupils at private schools is rising. | = student |
| qualification | *Qualifikation, Abschlusszeugnis* | I'm working hard to get my qualification "Fachschulreife". | |
| (to) qualify | *sich qualifizieren, geeignet machen* | | |
| qualified | *ausgebildet, qualifiziert* | Tony Green is a qualified carpenter ("Schreiner"). | |
| relationship | *Beziehung* | School trips help pupils to develop a better relationship with each other. | |
| (to) repeat | *wiederholen* | In Germany students who get bad results in their tests have to repeat a year. | |
| scared | *verängstigt* | Most kids are a bit scared when they start school. | = frightened |
| school fees | *Schulgeld, Schulgebühren* | At private schools pupils have to pay school fees of £10,000 a year or more. | |
| school holiday(s) | *Schulferien* | In my last school holidays I visited Argentina. | = vacation [AE] |
| school leaver | *Schulabgänger* | Young school leavers often turn to the careers officer for advice. | |
| school meal | *(Mittag-) Essen in der Schule* | Sally's favourite school meal is fish and chips. | = school lunch, school dinner |
| school trip | *Schulfahrt, Klassenreise* | Many parents say that school trips are too expensive. | = excursion |

| vocabulary | dt. Bedeutung | English sentence | syn/opp |
|---|---|---|---|
| school uniform | *Schuluniform* | At British schools nearly all children wear school uniforms. | |
| school yard | *Schulhof* | Students often fight in the school yard between lessons. | |
| school-leaving certificate | *Abgangszeugnis* | At 16 English school children receive their school-leaving certificate. | |
| secondary school [BE] | *höhere (weiterführende) Schule* | John Simpson was the first in his family to complete secondary school and go to university. | = high school [AE] |
| (to) sit a paper | *eine Klausur schreiben* | We had to sit a paper on the Glorious Revolution of 1688. | = (to) write a test |
| skill<br>skilled | *Fähigkeit, Fertigkeit*<br>*ausgebildet, qualifiziert* | At school young people learn lots of skills which will be useful for them in their jobs later on. | ≠ unskilled |
| (to) spell | *(richtig) schreiben, buchstabieren* | How do you spell this word, please? | |
| spelling | *Schreibung, Rechtschreibung* | Grandparents think that good spelling and grammar are more important than computer knowledge. | |
| state school | *staatliche Schule* | State schools are free for all children. | ≠ public school [BE] |
| (to) stay on | *länger in der Schule bleiben* | When they are 16 English pupils can leave school. Some stay on to take A-levels. | ≠ (to) drop out of |
| (to) study | *studieren* | Prince William studied History of Art ("Kunstgeschichte") in Scotland. | |

| vocabulary | dt. Bedeutung | English sentence | syn/opp |
|---|---|---|---|
| subject | *Schulfach* | Most pupils think that English and maths are difficult subjects. | |
| (to) take an exam | *eine Prüfung machen* | British school children take their first exam when they are 7. | |
| talent<br>talented | *Begabung*<br>*begabt* | Daniel has creative talent.<br>He wants to be an artist. | = gift<br>= gifted |
| term | *Trimester* | In England the school year has three terms: spring, summer and winter term. | |
| textbook | *Lehrbuch* | Unit 1 of our textbook is about radio programmes. | |
| training | *Ausbildung* | In England, many school leavers start a job without any training. | |
| training course | *Ausbildungskurs* | YTS offers training courses for school leavers who do not have a job. | |
| university | *Universität* | After school Mathew wants to go to Oxford University. | |
| vocabulary | *Wortschatz, Vokabular* | We have to take one vocabulary test every week. | |
| (to) worry | *sich sorgen* | Zoe worried about the result of her last English test. | |
| written test | *Klassenarbeit, schriftliche Arbeit* | I don't think I did very well in the last written test in physics. | ≠ oral exam |

# Leisure

| vocabulary | dt. Bedeutung | English sentence | syn/opp |
|---|---|---|---|
| activity | *(Freizeit-) Beschäftigung im Freien* | Gerry's favourite activity after school is cycling. | |
| adventure | *Abenteuer* | A helicopter flight over the Grand Canyon is quite an adventure. | |
| amusement | *Spaß, Unterhaltung* | My family's favourite amusement is playing Monopoly together. | |
| amusing | *unterhaltend* | | = enjoyable, pleasant |
| athletics | *Leichtathletik* | British children can practise athletics at school. | |
| (to) do athletics | *Leichtathletik betreiben* | Max has been doing athletics since he was twelve. | |
| audience | *Publikum, Zuschauer* | An international audience listened to the concerts at the Royal Albert Hall. | |
| (to) avoid | *vermeiden* | If you want to avoid mass tourism, go the west coast of Majorca. | |
| (to) celebrate | *feiern* | St. Patrick's Day is celebrated on March 17. | |
| celebration | *Feier, Fest* | | |
| cycling | *Rad fahren* | The Tour de France is the world's most important cycling event. | = riding a bike |
| (to) decide | *entscheiden* | As it was raining we decided to go to the museum. | |
| decision | *Entscheidung* | It was a good decision to stay out of the rain. | |
| destination | *Ziel* | It took us five hours to reach our destination. | |

| vocabulary | dt. Bedeutung | English sentence | syn/opp |
|---|---|---|---|
| (to) entertain<br>entertainment | *unterhalten*<br>*Unterhaltung* | The best TV programmes entertain and educate at the same time. | |
| event | *Ereignis* | Wimbledon lawn tennis is an important sport event in the United Kingdom. | |
| exercise<br><br><br>(to) exercise | *(körperliche) Bewegung, Training, Gymnastik*<br>*üben* | The doctor told Sandra to do more exercise. | |
| (to) explore<br><br>exploration | *erkunden, erforschen*<br>*Erforschung* | We explored the area around Loch Ness on bikes – but we didn't see the monster. | |
| fair | *Markt, Jahrmarkt* | We spent the day looking through books at the book fair. | |
| fashion | *Mode* | Fashions come and go. | |
| fashion magazine | *Modezeitschrift* | Liz Jones is the editor of fashion magazine Marie Claire. | |
| fashionable | *modisch* | Leo was wearing fashionable shoes. | |
| favourite | *Lieblings-* | Ibiza is my favourite island. | |
| festival | *Festspiel, Festival* | The Edinburgh festival takes place in August and September. | |
| (to) get away | *entfliehen, entkommen* | We always try to get away from the crowds – we prefer quieter places. | = (to) escape |
| (to) go (window) shopping | *(Schaufenster-) Bummel machen* | My aunt Mary likes to go window shopping. I hate it. | |
| (to) go for a walk | *einen Spaziergang machen* | Every Sunday my parents go for a walk. | |

| vocabulary | dt. Bedeutung | English sentence | syn/opp |
|---|---|---|---|
| gymnastics | *Turnen* | In gymnastics some world record holders are still at school. | |
| hip | *Hüfte* | Hip jeans were very popular last summer. | |
| indoor | *Hallen-* | Our hotel had a very nice indoor pool. | ≠ outdoor |
| indoors | *drinnen* | On cold days we stayed indoors. | ≠ outdoors |
| interest | *Interesse* | | |
| (to) be interested in | *Interesse haben an* | Most girls are interested in cosmetics and clothes. | |
| (to) keep fit | *fit, gesund bleiben* | My neighbour does aerobics three times a week to keep fit. | |
| latest | *neueste(r, s)* | Victoria is always dressed in the latest fashion. | |
| leisure centre | *Freizeitzentrum* | Moray Leisure Centre has a pool, a health centre and a coffee bar. | |
| (to) listen to CDs/to the radio | *CDs/Radio hören* | Ken's favourite pastime is listening to CDs. | |
| (to) look forward to | *sich freuen auf* | James and his sister Laura are looking forward to their exchange year. | |
| musician | *Musiker* | Bruce Springsteen started his career as a musician in bars and clubs. | |
| outdoor | *im Freien* | The camp at Whitstable offers a lot of outdoor activities. | ≠ indoor |
| (to) paint | *malen* | Dave painted the walls of his room blue and yellow. | |

| vocabulary | dt. Bedeutung | English sentence | syn/opp |
|---|---|---|---|
| pastime | *Zeitvertreib* | Playing video games is Alexander's favourite pastime. | |
| (to) perform<br>performance | *aufführen*<br>*Aufführung* | The drama group will perform their next play at our school in May. | = (to) stage |
| (to) phone friends | *Freunde anrufen* | Phoning your friends on a mobile can be very expensive. | = (to) call |
| (to) play a musical instrument | *ein Musikinstrument spielen* | I was ten when I started playing an instrument. | |
| (to) play chess | *Schach spielen* | Do you think that people who play chess are more intelligent? | |
| (to) play in a band | *in einer Band spielen* | Have you ever played in a school band? | |
| (to) play on the computer | *am Computer spielen* | Bob's mother thinks that her son spends too much time playing on his computer. | |
| popular<br>popularity | *beliebt*<br>*Beliebtheit* | Watching television is a very popular pastime. | |
| (to) relax | *sich entspannen* | The passengers could relax watching a film during the long flight. | |
| (to) ride a bike | *Fahrrad fahren* | Riding a bike is much healthier than going by car. | = (to) go cycling |
| (to) set out | *aufbrechen* | We set out for our mountain tour at 4 o'clock in the morning. | |
| sight | *Sehenswürdigkeit* | London has many interesting sights. | |

| vocabulary | dt. Bedeutung | English sentence | syn/opp |
|---|---|---|---|
| sightseeing<br>(to) go sight-seeing | *Besichtigungen*<br>*besichtigen* | During the sightseeing tour a guide told us all about the Great Fire of London (1666). | |
| spare time | *Freizeit* | Some managers cannot relax in their spare time. | = leisure, free time |
| spare-time activity | *Freizeitbeschäftigung* | For many young men sport is their most important spare-time activity. | |
| spectacular | *atemberaubend, fantastisch* | In Disney's Epcot Centre you can watch a spectacular laser show. | |
| stay | *Aufenthalt* | "Enjoy your stay", the hotel manager said. | |
| (to) stay at a hotel | *in einem Hotel wohnen* | Staying at a hotel is more expensive than camping. | |
| (to) surf the Internet | *im Internet surfen* | Surfing the internet for hours is cheaper today than it used to be. | |
| (to) take a break | *eine Pause machen* | On our bike tour we took a break by the riverside. | |
| (to) take part in | *teilnehmen an* | All students wanted to take part in the night excursion. | |
| (to) take place | *stattfinden* | In England, horse races take place at Newmarket, Epsom, Cheltenham and Aintree for example. | |
| tourist attraction | *Touristen-attraktion* | Orlando in Florida offers many tourist attractions. | |
| trainers | *Turnschuhe* | In 1979 Nike produced the first trainers with air in their soles. | |
| trendy<br>trend | *modisch*<br>*Trend, Richtung* | It was very trendy to wear a coloured plastic band on your wrist. | |

| vocabulary | dt. Bedeutung | English sentence | syn/opp |
|---|---|---|---|
| vacation [AE] | *Ferien* | Where are you going for your vacation? | = holiday [BE] |
| viewer | *Zuschauer* | Soap operas have more viewers than any other TV programme. | |
| (to) watch sport on TV | *Sport im Fernsehen sehen* | Luke shouldn't watch sport on TV only – he should go out and practise it. | |
| (to) watch television | *fernsehen* | Young kids and older people watch television for long hours every day. | |
| (to) wear | *(Kleidung) tragen* | In the 1950s and 60s women were not allowed to wear trousers in banks or offices. Today they can wear what they want. | |
| wristband | *Armband* | Lance Armstrong sold yellow wristbands for his cancer foundation ("Krebsstiftung"). | |
| youth centre | *Jugendhaus, Jugendheim* | The mayor promised the city would build a new youth centre. | |
| youth club | *Jugendclub* | Kevin and his friends meet at the local youth club to practise in the band. | |

# Sport

| vocabulary | dt. Bedeutung | English sentence | syn/opp |
|---|---|---|---|
| ability<br>(to) be able | *Fähigkeit*<br>*fähig sein, können* | In games people test their own ability against that of others. | = skill, talent<br>≠ inability |
| abroad | *ins, im Ausland* | Our team played abroad for the first time this year. | = overseas<br>≠ at home |
| achievement<br>(to) achieve | *Leistung*<br>*erreichen, leisten* | Some politicians think that the achievements of sportsmen show the success of a nation. | |
| activity<br><br><br>(to) act<br>action<br>active | *(Freizeit-) Beschäftigung im Freien, Tätigkeit*<br>*handeln*<br>*Handlung*<br>*aktiv, lebhaft* | In the summer Jennifer likes outdoor activities like riding her bike and canoeing. | ≠ inactivity |
| (to) admire<br>admiration | *bewundern*<br>*Bewunderung* | Who do you admire most: a pop star, a writer, a film star or a sportsman? | ≠ (to) hate |
| (to) adopt<br><br>adoption | *übernehmen, adoptieren*<br>*Annahme, Übernahme* | Cricket was adopted by many English-speaking countries around the world. | |
| aerobics<br>(to) do aerobics | *Aerobic*<br>*Aerobic machen* | My neighbour does aerobics three times a week to keep fit. | |
| against | *gegen* | Our next match will be against the present champions. | = versus |
| amateur | *Amateur* | An amateur practises his sport without receiving any money. | ≠ professional, pro |

| vocabulary | dt. Bedeutung | English sentence | syn/opp |
|---|---|---|---|
| angry<br>anger | *zornig*<br>*Zorn, Ärger, Wut* | The fans are angry because the best player of the team is going to join another club. | = furious, (to go) mad<br>≠ pleased |
| arrow | *Pfeil* | In archery ("Bogenschießen") they use bows and arrows. | |
| association | *Verband* | The English Football Association (FA) was created in 1863. | |
| (to) assume | *glauben, annehmen* | The fans assume that their club will win the league again this year. | = (to) suppose, (to) believe |
| (to) assure | *(jmdm. etwas) versichern* | The player assured that he had not handled the ball. | = (to) make sth. sure or certain |
| athlete | *Athlet* | The aim of any excellent athlete is to take part in the Olympic games. | = sportsman, sportswoman |
| athletics | *Leichtathletik* | British children can practise athletics at school. | |
| attack<br>(to) attack | *Angriff*<br>*angreifen* | The trainer said, "Attack is the best form of defence." | ≠ defence |
| (to) attend | *anwesend sein* | More than 95,000 people attended the final. | = (to) be present at |
| audience | *Zuschauer, Publikum* | Boxing always attracts a large TV audience. | |
| awful | *schrecklich* | After fouling his friend Jim, Harry felt awful. | = terrible |
| (to) behave | *sich benehmen* | Some youngsters just cannot behave on the sports grounds. | |
| (to) bet | *wetten* | The British like betting on horses and dogs. | |

| vocabulary | dt. Bedeutung | English sentence | syn/opp |
|---|---|---|---|
| boring | *langweilig* | Most people find fencing ("Fechten") boring. | |
| box office | *Kasse* | The box office will open at 6 o'clock. | |
| business | *Geschäft* | In the USA basketball is big business. | |
| (to) challenge<br>challenge | *herausfordern*<br>*Herausforderung* | The young boxer will challenge the title holder. | |
| champion | *Sieger/in, Champion* | In 1995 Michael Schumacher became the youngest Formula 1 World Champion. | |
| championship | *Meisterschaft* | In 1985 Boris Becker won the tennis championship at Wimbledon for the first time. | |
| (to) cheer | *anfeuern* | The spectators cheer their team. | |
| competition<br>(to) compete<br>competitive | *Wettbewerb*<br>*konkurrieren*<br>*konkurrenzfähig* | There is strong competition in professional sport. | |
| crowd | *Menge* | When David scored in the last minute the crowd went wild. | |
| defeat | *Niederlage* | The fans were very sad about the defeat of their football team. | ≠ victory, triumph |
| (to) defend<br>defence<br>defensive | *verteidigen*<br>*Verteidigung*<br>*abwehrend, rücksichtsvoll* | Boris Becker successfully defended his title at Wimbledon in 1986. | |
| (to) deserve | *verdienen* | Our team are playing very well today; I think they deserve to win. | |

| vocabulary | dt. Bedeutung | English sentence | syn/opp |
|---|---|---|---|
| (to) do sport | *Sport treiben* | You should do more sport to keep fit. | |
| draw | *Unentschieden* | Our last three matches ended in a draw. | |
| effort | *Anstrengung* | If you practise hard, your efforts will be rewarded. | |
| entertainment<br>(to) entertain | *Unterhaltung*<br>*unterhalten* | Sport has become a part of the entertainment industry. | |
| equipment<br>(to) equip | *Ausrüstung*<br>*ausstatten* | Excellent sportsmen get their equipment free from sponsors. | |
| (to) exercise | *trainieren, üben* | You will become better, if you exercise regularly. | = (to) train |
| fight<br>(to) fight | *Kampf*<br>*kämpfen* | In boxing, many fights are decided on points. | |
| final | *Endspiel* | If we win our next match, we'll reach the final. | |
| (to) gain | *erlangen, gewinnen* | In 1991, Boris Becker gained the title "World's Best Tennis Player". | = (to) win |
| (to) get rid of | *los werden* | Some people get rid of their aggression in sport. | |
| goalkeeper | *Torwart* | Our team has the best goalkeeper of the second division. | = goalie |
| ground | *Stadion* | FC Chelsea's home ground is Stamford Bridge. | = stadium |
| healthy<br>health | *gesund*<br>*Gesundheit* | Sport keeps your body fit and healthy! | ≠ unhealthy<br>≠ illness |
| hooligan | *Rowdy* | Young hooligans caused trouble at the matches. | |
| hooliganism | *Rowdytum* | How can we prevent football hooliganism? | |

| vocabulary | dt. Bedeutung | English sentence | syn/opp |
|---|---|---|---|
| (to) injure<br>injury | *verletzen*<br>*Verletzung* | Our best player is out for the rest of the season because he has injured his knee. | = (to) hurt |
| (to) last | *dauern* | A game of cricket lasts all day. | |
| manager | *Trainer* | The manager decided to buy a new goalkeeper from abroad. | = trainer, coach |
| match | *Spiel* | "Match of the Day" is a popular programme on British television. | = game |
| muscle | *Muskel* | In swimming you use more muscles in the body than in any other form of exercise. | |
| Olympic Games | *Olympische Spiele* | Many people consider the Olympic Games as big business. | |
| penalty | *Elfmeter, Strafstoß; Strafe* | David Beckham scored the penalty which decided the game. | |
| physical | *körperlich* | You have to do more physical exercise or you will get too fat! | ≠ mental |
| pitch | *Spielfeld* | Young fans threw beer cans onto the pitch. | = field, sports ground |
| pleasure<br>(to) please<br>pleasant | *Vergnügen*<br>*jmdm. gefallen*<br>*angenehm* | Very often the pleasure of sport gets lost when too much money is involved. | = joy, enjoyment, delight |
| popular<br>popularity | *beliebt*<br>*Beliebtheit* | Soccer is the most popular sport in England. | = well-liked<br>≠ unpopular |
| power<br>powerful | *Kraft, Stärke*<br>*kraftvoll* | The cheerleaders chanted, "We got power, we got style!" | = strength<br>≠ weakness |

| vocabulary | dt. Bedeutung | English sentence | syn/opp |
|---|---|---|---|
| prestige | *Ansehen* | As soon as the question of prestige arises, fair play disappears. | = status |
| professional | *Profi-, Berufs-(sportler)* | A professional football player can earn a lot of money in a couple of years. | ≠ amateur |
| record | *Rekord* | In 1996 the Brazilian footballer Ronaldo was sold to Barcelona for the record sum of $19.2 million. | |
| referee | *Schiedsrichter* | The referee stopped the match, because the players started to fight each other. | |
| reputation | *Ruf* | Because of the hooligans Britain's football fans have a bad reputation. | |
| riot | *(Straßen-) Schlacht* | There are often riots in the streets on the way to the stadium. | |
| rival | *Konkurrent* | Arsenal London and Manchester United are rivals. | = competitor<br>≠ partner |
| rule | *Bestimmung, Verbot, Vorschrift* | Games are played according to rules. | |
| (to) score a goal | *ein Tor schießen* | I have scored some goals! | |
| (to) shout | *schreien* | The girls shouted, "Our team will win!" | = (to) scream |
| (to) sign a contract | *einen Vertrag unterschreiben* | 18-year-old LeBron James signed a $90 million contract with Nike. | |
| soccer | *(europäischer) Fußball* | My girlfriend Zoe is not interested in soccer. | = football [BE] |
| spectator | *Zuschauer* | The spectators went wild when their club won the championship. | |

| vocabulary | dt. Bedeutung | English sentence | syn/opp |
|---|---|---|---|
| sport event | *Sportveranstaltung* | People go to watch sport events because they find them exciting. | |
| sportsman, sportswoman | *Sportler, Sportlerin* | Young Jonathan is a very good sportsman. | = athlete |
| stimulant | *Droge* | Sometimes sportsmen take stimulants to win. | = drug |
| success<br>(to) succeed<br>successful | *Erfolg*<br>*Erfolg haben*<br>*erfolgreich* | Success is a must for professional football clubs. | |
| supporter | *(Fußball-) Anhänger* | I've always been a keen supporter of our local football team. | = fan |
| tournament | *Turnier* | Wimbledon is the biggest tennis tournament in Britain. | |
| track (race track) | *(Renn-) Bahn* | Michael Schumacher was regarded as "King of the Race Track". | |
| (to) train<br>trainer<br>training | *trainieren*<br>*Trainer*<br>*Training* | An amateur works during the day and trains in his free time. | |
| (to) vandalise<br>vandalism | *zerstören*<br>*Zerstörungswut* | It's a shame that young people vandalise trains or buses. | = (to) destroy |
| victory<br>victorious | *Sieg*<br>*siegreich* | For many people victory is most important. | ≠ defeat |
| whistle<br><br>(to) whistle | *(Schiedsrichter-) Pfeife*<br>*pfeifen* | The referee blew his whistle to stop the game. | |
| world championship | *Weltmeisterschaft* | Franz Beckenbauer brought the 2006 football world championships to Germany. | |

# Health

| vocabulary | dt. Bedeutung | English sentence | syn/opp |
|---|---|---|---|
| addicted<br>addiction | *süchtig*<br>*Sucht* | Many people become addicted to alcohol. | |
| (to) admit | *zugeben, zugestehen* | Brian admitted that he had sold hash to young kids. | ≠ (to) deny |
| (to) affect | *sich auswirken auf, betreffen, in Mitleidenschaft ziehen* | Alcohol affects clear thinking and causes accidents. | |
| (to) arrest | *festnehmen, verhaften* | A 25-year-old man was arrested for selling drugs to school children. | ≠ (to) set free |
| available | *verfügbar* | In big cities drugs are available almost everywhere. | |
| average<br><br>on average | *Durchschnitts-, Durchschnitt*<br>*im Durchschnitt* | An average man needs 2,500 calories a day. | |
| balanced diet | *ausgewogene Ernährung* | If you eat meat, fish, milk, cheese and vegetables, you eat a balanced diet. | ≠ imbalanced diet |
| (to) ban<br>ban | *verbieten*<br>*Verbot* | Cigarettes are banned in public buildings. | ≠ (to) allow |
| beef | *Rindfleisch* | Hindus are not allowed to eat beef. They believe cows are sacred. | |
| (to) blame | *jmdm. die Schuld geben (an), jmdm. Vorwürfe machen (wegen)* | Doctors blame sugary foods for the weight problems which many young children have. | |
| (to) boil | *kochen, zum Kochen bringen* | Some of my school friends like cooking, others cannot even boil an egg. | |

| vocabulary | dt. Bedeutung | English sentence | syn/opp |
|---|---|---|---|
| bored<br>boredom | *gelangweilt sein, sich langweilen*<br>*Langeweile* | Some teenagers drink alcohol because they feel bored. | ≠ thrilled, excited |
| (to) borrow | *sich borgen, ausleihen* | My friend Jeff has borrowed a lot of money from his class mates. | |
| brain | *Gehirn* | Too much alcohol damages the brain and many other parts of the body. | |
| busy | *belebt, geschäftig* | Pubs are very busy at lunchtime. | |
| calorie | *Kalorie* | A large coke has 226 calories. | |
| cancer | *Krebs* | Tobacco smoke causes lung cancer. | |
| (to) cause | *verursachen* | Drugs and alcohol cause a lot of problems in families. | |
| cereals | *Frühstücks-zerealien (Cornflakes, Müsli)* | I have cereals for breakfast every day. | |
| chain | *Kette* | Wayne Molino works for the Primecut Hamburger chain. | |
| (to) check | *überprüfen, kontrollieren* | The police check pubs to make sure they are not selling alcohol to under-18s. | = (to) control |
| (to) connect<br>connection | *verbinden (mit)*<br>*Verbindung* | Teenagers often connect alcohol with the attractive things in life. | = (to) link, (to) combine ≠ (to) disconnect |
| (to) contain<br>contents | *enthalten*<br>*Inhalt* | Soft drinks contain a lot of sugar and make you fat. | |

| vocabulary | dt. Bedeutung | English sentence | syn/opp |
|---|---|---|---|
| (to) cook | *kochen, eine Mahlzeit zubereiten* | Today more men can cook at home than 30 years ago. | |
| cooking | *Essen, Mahlzeiten, Küche* | Many tourists do not like British cooking. | |
| crisps | *Chips* | Crisps are extremely unhealthy. | |
| customer | *Kunde* | Children are McDonald's best customers. | |
| dairy products | *Molkereierzeugnisse* | Dairy products – milk, butter, cheese, cream and yogurt – are good for your health. | |
| (to) damage | *schädigen* | Ecstasy pills damage brain cells. | ≠ (to) cure, (to) heal |
| (to) declare | *erklären, verkünden, bekanntmachen* | The president declared the White House a smoke-free zone. | |
| declaration | *Erklärung* | | |
| diet | *Kost, Ernährung, Nahrung* | Meat, fish, milk, cheese and vegetables are part of a healthy diet. | |
| (to) be on a diet, (to) go on a diet | *eine Schlankheitskur machen* | Cindy wants to lose weight – she's going on a diet. | |
| (to) digest<br>digestion | *verdauen*<br>*Verdauung* | The foods you eat are broken down, or digested, inside your body into smaller and smaller pieces. | |
| dinner | *Abendessen, Abendbrot* | We normally have dinner at half past seven. | |
| disease | *Krankheit* | Doctors can cure many diseases today. | = illness |
| dish | *Gericht* | Many British families eat international dishes. | = meal |

| vocabulary | dt. Bedeutung | English sentence | syn/opp |
|---|---|---|---|
| dish | *Schale, Schüssel, Platte* | Carla served the meal on beautiful dishes. | = plate |
| drug | *Droge, Rauschgift; Medikament* | Two of the biggest problems today are drugs and crime. | |
| eating disorder | *Essstörung* | Problems at home and at school can lead to eating disorders. | |
| (to) encourage | *ermutigen, jmdm. Mut zusprechen* | Adverts may encourage young people to start smoking. | ≠ (to) discourage |
| energy | *Energie* | The body changes the calories in food into energy. | |
| exercise<br>(to) get exercise | *Bewegung*<br>*sich bewegen* | Britons, on the whole, get far too little exercise. | ≠ (to) laze around |
| fashionable | *modisch, schick* | A lot of parents think that their children drink because they find it fashionable. | |
| fat | *Fett* | The fast food restaurants use less fat in their mayonnaise. | |
| fries | *Pommes* | Most people like ketchup with their fries. | = chips |
| habit | *Gewohnheit* | Think about your eating habits. Do you eat healthily? | |
| (to) harm | *schädigen* | Alcohol harms young people. | = (to) damage, (to) affect |
| harmful | *schädlich* | Smoking is extremely harmful. | = damaging |
| headache | *Kopfschmerzen* | Marc had terrible headache. I gave him two aspirins. | |
| health<br>healthy | *Gesundheit*<br>*gesund* | Too much fast food is bad for your health. | ≠ illness, disease |

| vocabulary | dt. Bedeutung | English sentence | syn/opp |
|---|---|---|---|
| hospital | *Krankenhaus* | The American tourist who was hit by a London bus was taken to St Stephen's hospital. | = clinic |
| illegal | *illegal, ungesetzlich, gesetzwidrig* | Cannabis, cocaine and heroin are illegal drugs. | ≠ legal, lawful |
| (to) improve | *verbessern, besser machen/werden* | The government wants to improve people's health. | ≠ (to) make worse |
| improvement | *Verbesserung* | | |
| junk food | *minderwertiges, ungesundes Essen* | The government wants to stop TV adverts for junk food. | ≠ healthy diet, healthy food |
| label | *Etikett* | Cigarette packages carry a warning label. | |
| lamb | *Lamm (-fleisch)* | In India a hamburger is made of lamb, because Hindus mustn't eat beef. | |
| lifestyle | *Lebensstil, Lebensweise* | A healthy lifestyle helps to avoid illness and suffering. | |
| lunch | *Mittagessen* | Anne worked as an au pair in England: she cleaned the house and cooked lunch and dinner for the family. | |
| meal | *Mahlzeit* | A large fast food meal has more than 1,300 calories. | |
| menu | *Speisekarte* | "Super size" meals are no longer on the menus of McDonald's in the UK. | |
| non-smoking zone (area) | *Nichtraucherbereich* | Many restaurants now have non-smoking zones. | |
| (to) offer | *anbieten* *Angebot* | Many young people under eighteen are offered their first alcohol at home. | |

| vocabulary | dt. Bedeutung | English sentence | syn/opp |
|---|---|---|---|
| (to) order | *bestellen* | In most fast food restaurants today you can order fresh fruit and salads. | |
| overweight | *übergewichtig* | Two thirds of British men are overweight. | ≠ underweight |
| (to) provide | *zur Verfügung stellen, liefern* | Fresh fruit, vegetables, milk, eggs and fish provide the body with protein, vitamins and minerals. | = (to) supply |
| (to) recommend<br>recommendation | *empfehlen*<br>*Empfehlung* | It is recommended that you do some exercise every day. | = (to) advise |
| (to) reduce<br>reduction | *verringern*<br>*Verringerung* | The food industry must reduce the fat content of fast food. | ≠ (to) increase |
| (to) restrict<br>restriction | *etwas beschränken, einschränken*<br>*Beschränkung* | Smokers' rights are becoming more and more restricted. | = (to) limit |
| (to) save | *sparen* | Mick could save a lot of money if he didn't smoke. | ≠ (to) spend, (to) waste |
| (to) shorten | *verkürzen* | Every cigarette you smoke shortens your life by seven to eleven minutes. | ≠ (to) lengthen, (to) make longer |
| soft drink | *alkoholfreies Getränk* | Coca Cola and Pepsi are soft drinks. | |
| strict | *streng* | Stricter regulations about smoking in public were introduced in New York. | |
| supper | *Abendessen* | My sister and I always wash the dishes after supper. | |
| (to) taste<br>taste<br>tasty | *schmecken*<br>*Geschmack*<br>*lecker* | This tomato soup tastes delicious. I think I'd like some more, please. | |

| vocabulary | dt. Bedeutung | English sentence | syn/opp |
|---|---|---|---|
| (to) treat<br>treatment | *behandeln*<br>*Behandlung* | Doctors diagnose and treat diseases. | |
| vegan [i:] | *Veganer* | People who eat no animal products are called vegans. | |
| vegetables | *Gemüse* | The doctor told Emily to eat more fruit and vegetables. | |
| vegetarian | *vegetarisch, Vegetarier* | Most restaurants offer vegetarian dishes for people who do not eat meat. | |
| volunteer<br>voluntary | *Freiwillige/r*<br>*freiwillig* | Many young people work in hospitals as volunteers because they want to help. | |
| waiter, waitress | *Kellner/in* | There are no waiters or waitresses in fast food restaurants. | |
| warn<br>warning | *warnen*<br>*Warnung* | The police warn people not to drink and drive. | |
| weight | *Gewicht* | Eating too much fat causes weight problems. | |
| (to) lose weight | *abnehmen* | If you eat less food than your body needs, you will lose weight.<br>Jennifer is much too fat. She should lose weight. | = (to) go on a diet<br>≠ (to) put on weight, (to) gain weight |
| (to) weigh | *wiegen* | | |
| worry<br>(to) worry | *Sorge, Kummer*<br>*sich sorgen* | Too many worries can make people ill. | |

# Work

| vocabulary | dt. Bedeutung | English sentence | syn/opp |
| --- | --- | --- | --- |
| advice<br>(to) advise | *Rat*<br>*raten* | Before you choose a job, get some expert advice. | |
| application | *Bewerbung* | I handed in my application for a job with Barclays Bank yesterday. | |
| application form | *Bewerbungsformular* | The secretary helped me to complete the application form. | |
| (to) apply for a job | *sich um eine Stelle bewerben* | After leaving school, Harry applied for a job with several firms. | |
| apprentice | *Lehrling, Auszubildender* | If you want to learn your job properly, you should start as an apprentice. | |
| apprenticeship | *Lehrzeit, Lehre* | During his apprenticeship Ed didn't earn a lot of money. | |
| assembly line | *Fließband* | On an assembly line, a car is put together one piece at a time. | = conveyor belt |
| bankrupt | *bankrott, zahlungsunfähig* | The firm went bankrupt because their product didn't sell any longer. | |
| blue-collar worker | *Arbeiter* | People who work in factories are sometimes called blue-collar workers. | ≠ white-collar worker, clerk |
| career | *berufliche Laufbahn, Karriere* | Do you think that a pupil has enough time to practise to have a career as a top sportsman? | |

| vocabulary | dt. Bedeutung | English sentence | syn/opp |
|---|---|---|---|
| careers adviser | *Berufsberater* | Your local careers adviser helps you find out about training programmes in your area. | = careers officer |
| careers officer | *Berufsberater* | A careers officer informed us about jobs at the airport. | |
| child labour | *Kinderarbeit* | Child labour is a big problem in poor countries: young children work in factories. | |
| choice<br>(to) choose | *Wahl*<br>*wählen* | What would you like to do? The choice is yours. | |
| commerce | *Handel, Verkehr* | Commerce between Germany and China has grown. | = business, trade |
| commuter<br>(to) commute | *Pendler*<br>*pendeln* | Commuters travel a long distance from home to work every day. | |
| company | *Firma* | The new video game will earn a lot of money for our company. | = business, firm |
| compatible | *passend* | Try to find a job which is compatible with your qualifications. | = suited<br>≠ incompatible, unsuited |
| conveyor belt | *Montageband, Fließband* | Tom Birch stands at a conveyor belt all day. | = assembly line |
| customer | *Kunde* | The firm won new customers abroad. | = client |
| CV (curriculum vitae) | *Lebenslauf* | CV is short for the Latin "curriculum vitae". | |
| (to) dismiss | *entlassen, jmdn. kündigen* | As the company had not made a profit the manager had to dismiss 120 people. | = (to) discharge, (to) sack, (to) fire<br>≠ (to) employ, (to) hire |

| vocabulary | dt. Bedeutung | English sentence | syn/opp |
|---|---|---|---|
| (to) earn one's living | *seinen Lebensunterhalt verdienen* | How do you earn your living? | |
| (to) employ | *beschäftigen, anstellen* | The two largest firms in our town employ more than a thousand people each. | = (to) hire ≠ (to) dismiss, (to) discharge |
| employee | *Arbeitnehmer, Angestellter* | This company has more than 20,000 employees. | = worker |
| employer | *Arbeitgeber* | The government is one of the largest employers in our country. | |
| employment | *Beschäftigung, Arbeit* | Lisa Adelman is looking for employment as a waitress. | ≠ unemployment |
| equal opportunities [Pl.] | *Chancengleichheit* | Today, women enjoy equal opportunities at work. | ≠ discrimination |
| factory | *Fabrik* | More people work in offices than in factories. | = works, shop, plant, mill |
| favourable | *positiv, günstig, sympathisch* | Large business firms use advertising to create a favourable "image". | |
| (to) fire | *jmdn. rausschmeißen* | The unsuccessful manager was fired by the directors. | = (to) hire |
| (to) fill a position | *eine Stelle besetzen* | IBM is looking for a university graduate to fill the position of sales manager. | |
| full-time | *Vollzeit, ganztägig, Ganztags-* | Mary and Sean have just got married and they both work full-time. | ≠ part-time |
| full-time job | *Vollzeit-, Ganztagsarbeit* | Linda Heinz gave up her full-time job with the NatWest Bank to spend more time with her baby daughter Laura. | ≠ part-time job |
| income | *Einkommen, Einkünfte* | Many people who work in the City of London have a high income. | |

| vocabulary | dt. Bedeutung | English sentence | syn/opp |
|---|---|---|---|
| industry | *Industrie (-zweig), Gewerbe* | The shipbuilding industry is in great trouble today. | |
| industrialist | *Industrieller* | | |
| industrial | *industriell* | | |
| interview | *Vorstellung (-sgespräch)* | Sharon drove to London for an interview with a manager of the Royal Bank of Scotland. | |
| job | *Beruf, Beschäftigung, Stellung* | Even after looking around for more than seven months, Edwin hasn't found a new job yet. | = employment, work, occupation |
| job centre | *Arbeitsamt* | Every morning there is a long queue of job hunters outside the job centre. | = labor office [AE], labour exchange |
| job interview | *Vorstellungsgespräch* | Before you go to a job interview try to get as much information as possible about the firm in question. | |
| job market | *Arbeitsmarkt* | What effect will computers have on the job market? | = labour market, employment market |
| job sharing | *Arbeitsplatzteilung, Stellenteilung* | Job-sharing is a way for two people to fill one job. Each person has a permanent part-time post. | |
| labour exchange | *Arbeitsamt* | Every morning Gerry goes to the labour exchange to find out about new job offers. | = job centre, labour office |
| (to) live on | *leben von* | The Harrisons have to live on a very small income. | |
| (to) maintain | *aufrechterhalten, bewahren* | The Ford motor company works hard to maintain the quality of its cars. | |
| maintenance | *Bewahrung* | | |

| vocabulary | dt. Bedeutung | English sentence | syn/opp |
|---|---|---|---|
| (to) manufacture<br>manufacturer<br>manufactured goods | *herstellen, fabrizieren*<br>*Fabrikant*<br>*Fertigwaren* | Chemists can manufacture substances that do not exist in nature.<br>Britain sold manufactured goods to her colonies. | = (to) make, (to) produce<br><br>= finished products |
| minimum wage | *Mindestlohn* | The minimum wage is often not enough to live on. | |
| model | *Modell, Mannequin* | Sue dreams of working as a fashion model. | |
| notice<br>(to) hand in one's notice<br>(to) give notice | *Kündigung*<br>*selbst kündigen*<br>*jmdm. kündigen* | Dan did not like his job at the airport so he handed in his notice.<br>To make production cheaper the company gave notice to 50 employees. | |
| without notice | *fristlos* | As he had stolen some tools from the shop floor, Angus McDowell was dismissed without notice. | |
| offer<br>(to) offer | *Angebot*<br>*anbieten* | Liam accepted the new job offer. | |
| order<br><br>(to) order | *Bestellung, Auftrag*<br>*bestellen* | We thank you for your order of 25 Macintosh computers. | |
| output | *Ausstoß, Arbeitsleistung* | The daily output of cars at the new plant in Leipzig has gone up to 950 units. | |
| overtime<br>(to) work overtime | *Überstunden*<br>*Überstunden machen* | Mr Growney likes working overtime, because with the extra money he can take his family on holiday. | |
| part-time | *Teilzeit-, Halbtags-* | Natalie has a part-time job because she has to look after her baby son. | ≠ full-time |

| vocabulary | dt. Bedeutung | English sentence | syn/opp |
|---|---|---|---|
| pay, payment | *Bezahlung, Lohn* | Vince Vaughn works as a security guard but his pay is rather low. | = wages, salary |
| perspective | *Aussicht, Ausblick* | School leavers with good marks have better perspectives of getting a job soon. | = chance, opportunity, possibility |
| plant | *Anlage, Werk* | At their plant in Dresden AMD produces microprocessors. | = works, factory, mill |
| position | *Stellung* | Ian Morris took up his position as Assistant Manager in January. | = post, job |
| (to) produce | *herstellen, erzeugen* | The Porsche plant produces thousands of cars every year. | = (to) make, (to) manufacture |
| production | *Herstellung* | | |
| productive | *produktiv, ertragreich, rentabel* | | ≠ unproductive |
| (to) promote | *(jmdn.) befördern* | Declan Murphy was promoted to Deputy Staff Manager. | |
| promotion | *Beförderung; Werbung* | The band went on promotion tour for their latest CD. | |
| prospect | *Aussicht* | Leaving school and starting work is an exciting prospect. | |
| (to) qualify | *sich eignen* | Debbie Winter studied three languages, so she could qualify as a translator. | = be suited for |
| qualification | *Eignung; Vorbildung* | If you do not have good qualifications, it is very hard to find a job | |
| (to) quit | *selbst kündigen* | Jamie quit her job as a kitchen help after nine days. | = (to) resign |

| vocabulary | dt. Bedeutung | English sentence | syn/opp |
|---|---|---|---|
| regular job | *eine feste Stelle haben* | Gregory has a regular job as a mechanic. | |
| (to) resign<br>resignation | *selbst kündigen*<br>*Kündigung* | The chairman will resign next month. | |
| (to) retire | *in Pension gehen, in Rente gehen, sich pensionieren lassen* | Workers retire at the age of 65. | |
| retirement | *Rente, Pension* | | |
| rise | *Lohnerhöhung* | | |
| (to) get a rise | *eine Lohnerhöhung bekommen* | Brian Kelly has just got a rise of 50 pounds a month. | |
| (to) run a firm | *eine Firma leiten* | Jim Goodwin has run his firm for 23 years now. | |
| salary | *Gehalt (Geld)* | In her new job, Donna Birch can earn a salary of £14,900 a year. | |
| shift | *Schicht, Arbeitsschicht* | All his life William Peel has been working night shift. | |
| skill<br>skilful | *Fertigkeit, Qualifikation*<br>*erfahren, geschickt* | Our course is for people who wish to improve their skills and knowledge. | |
| skilled worker | *Facharbeiter* | A skilled worker has greater chances of finding a good job. | ≠ unskilled worker |
| staff | *Belegschaft* | The director was pleased about the good work of the whole staff. | = workforce |
| staff manager | *Personalchef* | I'd like to talk to the staff manager about my complaint, please. | = manager of personnel |
| stressful | *anstrengend, aufreibend, stressig* | Many businessmen have a stressful job these days. | |

| vocabulary | dt. Bedeutung | English sentence | syn/opp |
|---|---|---|---|
| strike<br>(to) call a strike | *Streik*<br>*einen Streik ausrufen* | The General Workers' Union will call a strike. | |
| (to) sweat | *schwitzen* | In Pakistan, even young children have to work long hours, sweating in the terrible heat. | |
| sweatshop | *Ausbeutungsbetrieb* | a small factory in which people work in very bad conditions | |
| tool | *Werkzeug, Gerät* | If you want to repair this old car, you'll need the right tools. | |
| trade | *Handel, Handelsverkehr* | Trade between the US and Germany has increased. | = commerce, business |
| trade | *Beruf (im Handwerk)* | James Dyar told his son to learn a proper trade. | = job |
| by trade | *von Beruf* | Oliver McDonald is a mechanic by trade. | |
| trade union | *Gewerkschaft* | In the 19th century the first trade union was formed in England. | = labor union [AE] |
| trainee | *Praktikant, in der Ausbildung Stehender, Azubi, Lehrling* | Richard works as a trainee reporter for "The Global News". | |
| training | *Ausbildung* | When Pamela Hall started in her new job, she was first given computer training. | |
| unemployed | *arbeitslos* | Unemployed school leavers get help from the government. | = jobless, out of work |
| unemployment | *Arbeitslosigkeit* | Unemployment is one of the greatest problems today. | |

| vocabulary | dt. Bedeutung | English sentence | syn/opp |
|---|---|---|---|
| unskilled | *ungelernt, nicht ausgebildet* | Unskilled workers can lose their jobs quickly. | ≠ skilled |
| vacancy<br>vacant | *freie Stelle, offene Stelle*<br>*frei* | Martin Beadle, who is a trained carpenter, has been looking for a vacancy in his area for months. | |
| wage | *Lohn Arbeitslohn* | As a carpenter he gets a wage of 420 pounds a week. | = pay |
| weakness | *Schwäche* | Paul knows that maths is one of his weaknesses. | ≠ strength |
| white-collar worker | *Büroangestellte/r* | People who work in offices or banks are called white-collar workers. | = clerk<br>≠ blue-collar worker |
| work<br>(to) be out of work | *Arbeit*<br>*arbeitslos sein* | Being out of work makes people feel depressed. | |
| working condition | *Arbeitsbedingung* | The trade unions fight for better working conditions. | |
| (to) work shifts | *Schicht arbeiten* | In our printing plant, we work 24 hour shifts. | |
| workshop | *Arbeitsgemein-schaft; Werkstatt* | Are you interested in a workshop on computer programming? | |

# Minorities

| vocabulary | dt. Bedeutung | English sentence | syn/opp |
|---|---|---|---|
| (to) abandon | *aufgeben, preisgeben, verlassen* | We must not abandon people who live in slums. | = (to) leave alone |
| (to) abolish | *abschaffen* | Slavery was abolished in the US in 1865. | |
| abolitionist | *Gegner der Sklaverei (auch der Todesstrafe)* | People who worked to end slavery were called abolitionists. | |
| admission<br>(to) admit | *Zulassung, Eintritt*<br>*zulassen, zugeben, zugestehen* | The admission of nine black students to an all-white High School caused trouble. | |
| adventure | *Abenteuer* | Many immigrants came to America looking for adventure. | |
| afraid<br>(to) be afraid | *verängstigt*<br>*befürchten* | White house owners were afraid that blacks would move into the neighbourhood. | |
| (to) allow<br>allowance | *erlauben*<br>*Erlaubnis* | Only foreign workers with qualifications are allowed into the country. | = (to) permit |
| ancestor | *Vorfahr* | Most Americans have ancestors who came from overseas. | ≠ descendant |
| annual | *jährlich, Jahres-* | The annual number of immigrants to the US is 290,000. | = yearly |
| anxiety | *Angst, Besorgnis* | Anxiety about jobs is not unusual among young black people. | = worry, concern |

| vocabulary | dt. Bedeutung | English sentence | syn/opp |
|---|---|---|---|
| anxious | *besorgt* | Jessica was anxious about getting a new job. | |
| appearance<br>(to) appear | *Erscheinung, Aussehen*<br>*erscheinen* | The neighbours were shocked by the appearance of their new neighbours. | = looks |
| area | *Gebiet, Bereich* | More Hispanics moved into the Miami area. | = district |
| (to) argue | *argumentieren; streiten* | He argues that immigrants prefer to live together in the same areas. | |
| argument | *Argument; Wortwechsel, Streit* | Many arguments against immigration are not justified. | |
| (to) arise | *sich ergeben, entstehen* | Problems arise when people do not trust each other. | = (to) develop, (to) start |
| (to) arrive<br>arrival | *ankommen*<br>*Ankunft* | The first Europeans arrived in the Americas in 1492. | ≠ (to) leave, (to) depart |
| ashamed | *beschämt* | Manuel felt ashamed because his parents were very poor. | ≠ proud |
| (to) ask for | *bitten* | Poor people are often too ashamed to ask for help. | |
| attitude | *Haltung, Einstellung* | Attitudes towards immigration are changing. | = view, opinion |
| (to) attract<br>attraction<br>attractive | *anziehen*<br>*Anziehungskraft*<br>*anziehend* | Many states tried to attract settlers. | |
| average<br><br>on average | *Durchschnitt, Durchschnitts-*<br>*im Durchschnitt, durchschnittlich* | The average immigration increased in the 19th century. | |
| baggage [AE] | *Gepäck* | The emigrants went on board carrying their baggage on their backs. | = luggage [BE] |

| vocabulary | dt. Bedeutung | English sentence | syn/opp |
|---|---|---|---|
| because of | *wegen* | Fewer immigrants came to the US in the 1960s because of new, stricter laws. | = due to |
| (to) belong | *gehören (zu), angehören* | A mixed marriage is a marriage in which partners belong to different races or religions. | |
| below | *unter, unten* | More blacks than whites live below the poverty line. | ≠ above |
| (to) blame | *die Schuld geben* | Some people blame foreigners for their own problems. | |
| border | *Grenze* | Illegal immigrants are caught at the US-Mexican border. | = frontier |
| burden | *Last* | Many Americans believe immigrants are a financial burden on the country. | |
| by birth | *von Geburt* | Wernher von Braun became an American citizen but he was German by birth. | |
| (to) cause<br>cause | *verursachen*<br>*Grund, Anlass* | Too many immigrants may cause unrest in a country. | = (to) bring about, (to) produce |
| century | *Jahrhundert* | The 19th century was a time of great industrial growth in the United States. | |
| citizen | *Staatsbürger* | Until 1971 Commonwealth citizens could settle freely in the UK. | |
| civil right | *Bürgerrecht* | An important civil right is the right to vote. | |

| vocabulary | dt. Bedeutung | English sentence | syn/opp |
|---|---|---|---|
| civil rights movement | *Bürgerrechtsbewegung (in den USA)* | Martin Luther King was the most important leader of the civil rights movement. | |
| clash | *Zusammenstoß* | Clashes between police and black immigrants took place in Los Angeles. | = riot, battle |
| community | *Gemeinde, Gemeinschaft* | New York City has the largest Jewish community in the world. | |
| concerned | *besorgt, betroffen* | American workers are concerned about the competition of cheap labour. | = worried |
| (to) criticize<br>criticism<br>critic | *kritisieren*<br>*Kritik*<br>*Kritiker* | Civil rights leaders criticized the new immigration law. | ≠ (to) praise |
| (to) deny<br>denial | *verweigern, leugnen*<br>*Ablehnung, Leugnen* | We mustn't deny anybody the right to vote. | ≠ (to) grant, (to) give |
| descendant | *Nachfahre* | Descendants of immigrants visit Ellis Island since it opened as a museum. | ≠ ancestor |
| desperate | *verzweifelt* | In the 19th century people in Ireland lived in desperate conditions. | |
| (to) differ<br>difference<br>different | *sich unterscheiden*<br>*Unterschied*<br>*verschieden* | Today's immigrants differ from Americans who have lived in the USA for a long time. | |
| disadvantage | *Nachteil* | Black children had to face more disadvantages than white children. | ≠ advantage |
| (to) be at a disadvantage | *benachteiligt sein* | In traditional societies, women are at a disadvantage. | |

| vocabulary | dt. Bedeutung | English sentence | syn/opp |
| --- | --- | --- | --- |
| disagreement<br>(to) disagree | *Uneinigkeit*<br>*nicht zustimmen* | The Puritans left England because of disagreements with the Church of England. | ≠ agreement |
| discrimination<br><br><br>(to) discriminate | *unterschiedliche Behandlung, Benachteiligung*<br>*benachteiligen* | Discrimination between men and women at work is against the law. | ≠ equality, equal opportunities |
| Ellis Island | *Insel vor New York, von 1892 bis 1943 Kontrollstelle für Einwanderer* | In the 19th and the 20th century 17 million immigrants arrived at Ellis Island. | |
| (to) emigrate<br><br>emigration<br>emigrant | *auswandern*<br><br>*Auswanderung*<br>*Auswanderer(in)* | The "Mayflower" was full of people who wanted to emigrate to America. | ≠ (to) immigrate<br>≠ immigration<br>≠immigrant |
| equal<br>equality<br>equal opportunities [Pl.]<br>equal pay | *gleich*<br>*Gleichheit*<br>*Chancengleichheit*<br>*gleiche Bezahlung* | All men are created equal.<br><br>Many blacks do not enjoy equal opportunities at work. | ≠ unequal<br>≠ inequality<br>≠ discrimination |
| ethnic<br><br>ethnic minority | *Volks-*<br><br>*Volksminderheit, ethnische Minderheit* | There are a lot of different ethnic groups in the USA.<br>The two largest ethnic minority groups in Britain are the Asians and Blacks. | |
| explorer<br>(to) explore<br>exploration<br>exploratory | *Forscher*<br>*erforschen*<br>*Erforschung*<br>*Forschungs-* | The explorer Christopher Columbus discovered the New World in 1492. | |
| ferry | *Fähre* | A ferry transported the immigrants from Ellis Island to New York. | |
| flight<br>(to) flee | *Flucht*<br>*fliehen* | People went to America in flight from poverty. | |

| vocabulary | dt. Bedeutung | English sentence | syn/opp |
|---|---|---|---|
| foreign | *ausländisch* | Do we need more foreign workers? | = from abroad, overseas |
| foreigner | *Ausländer* | | = alien |
| fortune | *Vermögen; Schicksal* | Gold-digger Norman Felt made a fortune in Alaska. | |
| fortunate | *glücklich, vom Schicksal begünstigt* | | = lucky |
| founding fathers | *Gründerväter* | The founding fathers of the United States were men like Franklin, Jefferson and Washington. | |
| frontier | *Grenze, Grenzgebiet* | The frontier is the borderline between civilization and wilderness. | |
| green card | *Aufenthaltserlaubnis* | A green card allows you to stay in the US and work. | |
| (to) guard<br>guard | *bewachen*<br>*Wächter* | The coasts and borders of the US are guarded day and night. | = (to) control |
| hate<br>(to) hate | *Hass*<br>*hassen* | The masses living in the black ghettos develop feelings of hate. | = hatred<br>≠ love |
| heritage<br>(to) inherit<br>hereditary | *Erbe*<br>*erben*<br>*Erb-* | Americans are proud of their heritage. | |
| Hispanics | *Hispano-Amerikaner* | Hispanics are America's largest minority. | = people from Spanish-speaking countries |
| homeland | *Heimatland, Vaterland* | Many Jamaicans left their homeland because they couldn't find any work. | = mother country |
| homeless | *obdachlos, Obdachlose(r)* | Can the government solve the problem of the homeless and poor? | = people without a roof over their heads |

| vocabulary | dt. Bedeutung | English sentence | syn/opp |
|---|---|---|---|
| hostility | *Feindschaft, Feindseligkeit* | Hostility between Italian and Polish immigrants increased. | ≠ friendship |
| hostile | *feindlich* | | ≠ friendly |
| human rights | *Menschenrechte* | The basic human rights are the right of life and liberty. | |
| illegal | *ungesetzlich, rechtswidrig* | It is illegal to enter the US without documents. | ≠ legal, lawful |
| immigrant | *Einwanderer* | Many immigrants came to the US in search of freedom. | ≠ emigrant |
| immigrant labour | *zugewanderte Arbeitskräfte* | The American workers face competition from cheap immigrant labour. | |
| (to) immigrate | *einwandern* | After 1820, more people began to immigrate. | ≠ (to) emigrate |
| immigration | *Einwanderung* | | ≠ emigration |
| immigration law | *Einwanderungsgesetz* | A new immigration law was passed by Congress. | = immigration bill/act |
| (to) increase | *steigern, erhöhen, zunehmen* | In 1990 the US government announced a plan to increase immigration. | ≠ (to) decrease, (to) reduce, (to) limit |
| increase | *Erhöhung, Zunahme* | The population increase in 1900 was due to millions of immigrants who entered the country at that time. | |
| increasing | *zunehmend, steigend* | | |
| (to) intimidate | *einschüchtern, bange machen* | Illegal workers can be intimidated easily. | = (to) scare, (to) frighten |
| jealous | *eifersüchtig* | Many neighbours were jealous of the successful Asian immigrant. | |
| jealousy | *Eifersucht* | | |
| journey | *Reise* | From 1882 to 1902 more than two million immigrants made the journey from Bremen to New York. | |
| language | *Sprache* | Foreigners must learn the language of the country they emigrate to. | |

| vocabulary | dt. Bedeutung | English sentence | syn/opp |
|---|---|---|---|
| (to) leave | *verlassen* | He had to leave the country within 72 hours. | = (to) get out of, (to) exit |
| liberty | *Freiheit* | The Statue of Liberty was a present of the French people to the Americans. | = freedom |
| (to) limit | *begrenzen* | A new law limits the number of newcomers. | = (to) restrict |
| low-paid job | *schlecht bezahlte Arbeit* | Many immigrants had to take low-paid jobs. | |
| majority | *Mehrheit* | The majority of the immigrants came to start a new life. | ≠ minority |
| melting pot | *Schmelztiegel* | Americans liked to believe that their country was a melting pot of nations. | |
| migration | *(Völker-) Wanderung* | The migration of black Americans to the cities in the North began after World War II. | |
| minority | *Minderheit* | The United Kingdom has a large black minority. | ≠ majority |
| misery | *Elend, Not* | Racial conflicts brought misery to many families. | = unhappiness |
| mix | *Mischung* | The modern nation is a mix of cultures and races. | |
| (to) mix | *mischen* | | |
| mixture | *Mischung, Gemisch* | Britain today is a curious mixture of past and present. | |
| mixed neighbourhood | *gemischte Wohngegend* | We live in a mixed neighbourhood. Our neighbours are from India, Pakistan and Jamaica. | |
| multi-racial | *aus vielen Rassen bestehend* | The US is a multi-racial society. | |

| vocabulary | dt. Bedeutung | English sentence | syn/opp |
|---|---|---|---|
| native | *einheimisch (Ur-) Einwohner* | The American Indians are the native population of the US. | |
| native Americans | *US Indianer* | Native Americans is the politically correct term for the Indian population in the US. | |
| newcomer | *Neuankömmling* | Many newcomers did not find what they had expected. | = a person who has recently arrived |
| neighbourhood | *Nachbarschaft* | The whites did not want blacks to move into their neighbourhood. | |
| nightmare | *Alptraum* | For many immigrants life in the US began like a nightmare. | = an unpleasant and terrible dream |
| non-violent | *gewaltlos* | M. L. King always supported non-violent resistance. | ≠ violent |
| (to) object to | *Einspruch erheben gegen* | The Pilgrims objected to some of the beliefs of the Church of England. | ≠ (to) approve of, (to) agree to |
| (to) oppose | *sich wenden gegen, gegen etwas sein* | The northern states began to oppose slavery. | ≠ (to) agree to, (to) accept |
| opposition | *Widerstand* | The new law met with a lot of opposition. | ≠ approval |
| opposite | *das Gegenteil; gegenüber, entgegengesetzt* | Hate is the opposite of love. The immigration office can be found in the opposite building. | |
| oppressed<br>oppression | *unterdrückt*<br>*Unterdrückung* | "We must fight for the oppressed people everywhere." | = suppressed, persecuted |
| outlaw | *Geächteter, Vogelfreier* | The outlaw Jesse James formed a gang. | = bandit, criminal |

| vocabulary | dt. Bedeutung | English sentence | syn/opp |
|---|---|---|---|
| (to) overcome | *überwinden, bewältigen* | Most immigrants managed to overcome their problems. | |
| (to) persecute | *verfolgen* | People who felt persecuted left their homelands. | |
| persecution | *Verfolgung* | Jews fled from persecution. | |
| pilgrim | *Pilger* | The Pilgrim Fathers sailed on board the Mayflower from Plymouth (England) to the New World. | |
| populated<br>(to) populate | *bevölkert*<br>*bevölkern* | Brixton, a district in South London, is populated mainly by black people. | = inhabited |
| population | *Bevölkerung* | London has a population of about nine million | |
| poverty | *Armut* | German farmers went to America to escape from poverty. | ≠ riches, wealth |
| poor | *arm* | | ≠ rich, wealthy |
| prejudice | *Vorurteil* | It's not only older people who have prejudices against foreigners. | |
| (to) be prejudiced against | *Vorurteile haben gegenüber* | Too many people are still prejudiced against foreigners. | |
| prospect | *Aussicht, Chance* | The immigrant had the prospect of earning a living for himself and his family. | = chance, hope |
| pursuit | *Streben, Trachten* | The US Declaration of Independence guarantees the pursuit of happiness. | |
| questionnaire | *Fragebogen* | The immigrants had to fill in a questionnaire. | |
| race | *Rasse* | Different races are living together in the same district. | |

| vocabulary | dt. Bedeutung | English sentence | syn/opp |
|---|---|---|---|
| race relations | *Rassen-beziehungen* | The problem of unemployment has made race relations worse in the last few years. | |
| racial | *rassisch, Rassen-* | Malcolm X believed that racial justice for blacks could be achieved. | |
| racial problem | *Rassenproblem* | There are still serious racial problems in Britain today. | = racial conflict |
| racial segregation | *Rassentrennung* | The Supreme Court decided that racial segregation in schools is against the constitution. | = separation, discrimination<br>≠ integration |
| racial tension | *Rassenspannung* | Racial tension between blacks and Asian immigrants increased. | |
| racism | *Rassismus* | Black Americans fought to end racism. | |
| racist | *Rassist* | Four black schoolgirls were killed by a white racist. | |
| refugee | *Flüchtling* | When people first come to a country they are often taken to a refugee camp. | |
| resistance<br>(to) resist<br>resistant | *Widerstand*<br>*sich widersetzen*<br>*widerstandsfähig* | M. L. King used Gandhi's method of non-violent resistance. | = opposition |
| respect<br>respected<br>respectable | *Achtung, Respekt*<br>*geachtet*<br>*anständig* | M. L. King won the respect of many white Americans. | |
| respect<br>respective, respectively | *Hinsicht, Beziehung*<br>*beziehungsweise* | In one respect, emigrating to America was very different from moving from one country to another in Europe. | |
| restriction | *Ein-, Beschränkung* | Canada introduced restrictions on the number of immigrants. | = limitation |

| vocabulary | dt. Bedeutung | English sentence | syn/opp |
| --- | --- | --- | --- |
| (to) restrict<br>restrictive | *beschränken*<br>*einschränkend* | | = (to) limit |
| riot | *(Straßen-) schlacht, Krawall* | Riots broke out after Martin Luther King was shot. | = fight, clash |
| rival | *Konkurrent* | Newcomers were often seen as rivals. | = competitor<br>≠ partner |
| scared<br>(to) scare | *verängstigt*<br>*erschrecken* | In some cities older people are scared to leave their homes after dark. | = frightened, afraid<br>= (to) frighten |
| search<br>(to) search | *Suche*<br>*suchen* | People have always come to America in search of riches. | |
| segregation | *Rassentrennung* | Racial segregation is against the constitution. | = separation<br>≠ integration |
| (to) separate [eit] | *trennen, (ab)teilen* | Black children and white children were separated at school. | |
| separate [it] | *getrennt, abgesondert* | Black and white children went to separate schools. | |
| (to) settle | *sich niederlassen; besiedeln* | The first English immigrants settled at Jamestown, Virginia, in 1607. | |
| settler | *Siedler* | The Pilgrim Fathers were the first settlers. | |
| settlement | *Siedlung, Niederlassung* | The settlement was surrounded by a fence. | |
| shelter<br>(to) shelter | *Schutz, Schutzraum*<br>*schützen* | Poor blacks do not have enough food, clothing, and shelter. | = house, roof, protection<br>= (to) protect |
| skill<br>skilled | *Fähigkeit, Fertigkeit*<br>*gelernt* | Immigrants brought new skills with them.<br>Skilled workers are always welcome. | |
| slavery | *Sklaverei* | Thousands of native Americans were killed in wars or forced into slavery. | ≠ freedom, liberty |

| vocabulary | dt. Bedeutung | English sentence | syn/opp |
|---|---|---|---|
| (to) slow down | *verringern, verlangsamen* | The Immigration Bill of 1971 slowed down the immigration of people from Commonwealth countries in Britain. | ≠ (to) speed up |
| society<br>social | *Gesellschaft*<br>*gesellschaftlich* | There are too many poor people in our modern society. | |
| social worker | *Sozialarbeiter* | Social workers try to help young people in trouble. | |
| (to) spread | *ausbreiten, verteilen* | The Indians spread across North and South America. | |
| standard of living | *Lebensstandard* | Americans enjoy a high standard of living. | |
| (to) sweat | *schwitzen* | Black slaves sweated on the plantations. | |
| (to) tackle | *fertig werden mit, anpacken (ein Problem)* | How will the president tackle the problem of the homeless and poor? | = (to) cope with |
| tension<br>tense | *Spannung*<br>*gespannt, spannend* | Racial tension between blacks and whites in Brixton has increased. | |
| (to) threaten<br>threat | *bedrohen*<br>*Bedrohung* | American jobs were threatened by cheap immigrant workers. | |
| tolerance<br><br>tolerant<br>(to) tolerate | *Duldsamkeit, Duldung*<br>*duldsam*<br>*dulden* | People should show more tolerance towards foreigners. | |
| (to) treat<br>treatment | *behandeln*<br>*Behandlung* | Undocumented immigrants were treated badly. | |
| tribe | *(Volks-) Stamm* | The Havasupai tribe lived in the Grand Canyon region. | |

| vocabulary | dt. Bedeutung | English sentence | syn/opp |
|---|---|---|---|
| trouble | *Problem, Schwierigkeit* | African Americans had trouble finding work. | = problem |
| undocumented | *ohne gültige Papiere* | Undocumented workers will now get a new chance to stay in the USA. | = illegal<br>≠ legal |
| unwanted | *unerwünscht, störend* | Some immigrants felt unwanted. | |
| victim | *Opfer* | A new website helps victims of bullying. | |
| violent | *gewalttätig; heftig* | Violent clashes between blacks and whites broke out last week. | ≠ non-violent |
| violence | *Gewalt, Gewalttätigkeit* | Problems cannot be solved by violence. | ≠ non-violence |
| welfare [AE] | *Sozialhilfe* | Many poor people in the US have to live on welfare. | = income support |
| work permit | *Arbeitserlaubnis* | If you want to work in the US, you need a work permit. | |
| (to) worry about | *sich Sorgen machen über* | Many Londoners worry about their safety on the Underground. | |
| xenophobia | *Ausländerfeindlichkeit* | We must try to overcome all sorts of xenophobia. | |

# Media

| vocabulary | dt. Bedeutung | English sentence | syn/opp |
|---|---|---|---|
| actor, actress | *Schauspieler, Schauspielerin* | J. K. Rowling helped choose the actors for the first Harry Potter film. | |
| (to) advertise | *inserieren, werben* | People advertise in newspapers to sell houses or used cars. | |
| advertisement (ad or advert) | *Anzeige* | Advertisements make up a large part of newspapers and magazines. | |
| advertising campaign | *Werbekampagne, Werbefeldzug* | McDonald's started a new advertising campaign to improve its image. | |
| advice column | *Ratgeberrubrik, -spalte (in Zeitschriften)* | A new advice column on our website offers answers to teenage problems. | |
| article | *Artikel* | I read an article about bike riders who died after taking drugs. | |
| audience | *Zuschauer, Publikum* | American football always has a large TV audience. | = viewers |
| BBC | *(British Broadcasting Corporation) TV Sender in Großbritannien* | The BBC was founded in 1922. | |
| box office | *Kino-, Theaterkasse* | Tom Hank's new film is a great box office success. | |
| (to) broadcast | *senden, übertragen* | The cup final will be broadcast live on television. | = (to) transmit, (to) show |
| brochure | *Broschüre* | I sent for a brochure about the Universal Studios. | = leaflet |
| cable TV | *Kabelfernsehen* | Cable TV uses wires instead to transmit signals. | |

| vocabulary | dt. Bedeutung | English sentence | syn/opp |
|---|---|---|---|
| cast | *Besetzung (in einem Film)* | The cast of the latest Steven Spielberg film was interviewed by reporters. | |
| CCTV | *(Abk.: Closed-circuit television) Video-überwachung* | The police use closed-circuit television (CCTV) to keep watch on shops and city centres. | |
| censorship | *Zensur* | In a free state there is no censorship. | |
| channel | *(Fernseh-) Kanal, Programm* | Most TV channels are financed by advertising. | |
| (to) choose<br>choice | *auswählen*<br>*Wahl* | On MTV kids choose the coolest singer by voting online. | |
| column | *(Zeitungs-) Spalte* | David Beckham wrote a column for the "Manchester Standard". | |
| commercial | *Werbesendung, -spot* | TV commercials are often quite funny. | |
| (to) communicate<br>communication | *etwas mitteilen*<br>*Kommunikation* | Today people communicate by phone and e-mail. | |
| contents<br>(to) contain | *Inhalt*<br>*enthalten* | The contents of the next Harry Potter book is still a secret. | |
| copy | *(Zeitungs-) Exemplar* | The British newspapers sell about 14 million copies every Sunday. | |
| cover | *Bucheinband* | Mary GrandPré designed the cover for the American edition of Harry Potter. | |
| (to) cover<br>coverage | *berichten über*<br>*Bericht* | The journalist covered many important events such as the Vietnam War or the fall of the Berlin Wall. | |

| vocabulary | dt. Bedeutung | English sentence | syn/opp |
|---|---|---|---|
| crew | *Besatzung, Mannschaft* | When the filming was finished the director invited the whole crew out for a meal. | |
| daily (newspaper) | *Tageszeitung* | Many Britons read more than one daily (newspaper). | ≠ weekly, monthly |
| dish, satellite dish | *Satellitenschüssel* | A dish picks up radio and TV signals from a satellite. | |
| (to) distribute<br>distribution | *verteilen*<br>*Verteilung, Vertrieb* | Books are distributed through bookstores or book clubs. | |
| (to) edit | *herausgeben, bearbeiten* | | |
| editor | *Redakteur, Herausgeber* | a journalist who is responsible for the final version of a text | |
| edition | *Auflage (= Nachdruck)* | This is the second edition of the *Vocabulary Exercises*. | |
| edition | *Ausgabe* | The first edition of the Gutenberg Bible was printed in 1451/52. | |
| encyclopaedia | *(sehr großes) Lexikon* | The Encyclopaedia Britannica gives information on many different subjects. | |
| entertainment<br>(to) entertain | *Unterhaltung*<br>*unterhalten* | Films, TV shows, and video games are different forms of entertainment. | |
| extract<br>(to) extract | *Auszug*<br>*herausholen* | I listened to a short extract from my favourite group's latest CD. | |
| feature | *Reportage, Beitrag* | Last night I watched an interesting feature on TV about hurricanes. | = report |

| vocabulary | dt. Bedeutung | English sentence | syn/opp |
|---|---|---|---|
| feedback | *Rückmeldung* | The TV companies ask viewers for feedback. | |
| freedom of expression | *Meinungsfreiheit* | Freedom of expression is the right to say what you think. | |
| freedom of the press | *Pressefreiheit* | A democratic government protects the freedom of the press. | |
| front page | *Titelseite* | The news about the tropical storm appeared on the front page of all papers. | |
| heading | *Überschrift* | Try to find a new heading for this paragraph. | = headline |
| headline | *Schlagzeile* | The marriage of the pop star made the headlines in many newspapers. | |
| importance<br>important | *Bedeutung, Wichtigkeit*<br>*wichtig* | Film and pop stars know about the great importance of the media. | |
| index | *Register* | An index is an alphabetical list printed at the back of a book. | |
| issue<br>(to) issue | *(Zeitungs-) Ausgabe, Nummer*<br>*herausgeben* | In our next issue we'll publish a full report on the latest computer video games. | |
| (to) launch | *starten; mit etwas beginnen* | The government is launching a new anti-smoking campaign. | = (to) start, (to) begin |
| letter to the editor | *Leserbrief* | I always read the letters to the editor in "The Times". | |
| live [ai] | *direkt* | The landing on the moon was shown live on TV. | ≠ (pre) recorded |
| manual | *Handbuch* | Read the instruction manual before trying out the new MP3 player. | |

| vocabulary | dt. Bedeutung | English sentence | syn/opp |
|---|---|---|---|
| mass media | *Massenmedien* | The mass media – television, radio, the newspapers – plays an important role in every society. | |
| message | *Nachricht, Botschaft, Mitteilung* | On our website you can read other people's messages. | |
| mysterious<br>mystery | *rätselhaft, geheimnisvoll*<br>*Geheimnis* | Hollywood made a film about the mysterious death of the Egyptian pharaoh Tutankhamen. | |
| national paper | *überregionale, d. h. im ganzen Land gelesene Zeitung* | The national papers in Britain sell about 13 million copies on weekdays. | ≠ regional paper, local paper |
| network | *Netz, Netzwerk* | Our firm has a computer network which allows all users to share information. | |
| news | *Nachricht(en)* | Have you heard the news today? | |
| paragraph | *(Text-) Absatz* | Try to summarize each paragraph in one sentence. | |
| (to) persuade<br>persuasion | *überzeugen, überreden*<br>*Überredung* | Big companies advertise to persuade people to buy their products. | |
| (to) print<br>print | *drucken*<br>*Druck* | Gutenberg invented the technique of printing in the 1450s. | |
| bold print<br>out of print | *Fettdruck*<br>*vergriffen (z. B. ein Buch)* | | ≠ small print |
| programme | *Sendung* | The BBC produces special programmes for children and young adults. | = show |

| vocabulary | dt. Bedeutung | English sentence | syn/opp |
|---|---|---|---|
| (to) promote<br>promotion | *fördern, für etwas werben*<br>*Werbung, Werbekampagne* | Music companies use the media to promote sales of CDs and music videos. | |
| (to) prosecute<br>prosecution | *gerichtlich verfolgen*<br>*Verfolgung* | PC users who download films from the Internet without paying will be prosecuted. | |
| (to) publish<br>publication | *veröffentlichen, herausgeben*<br>*Veröffentlichung* | Aspyr Media published a computer game based on the popular Lord of the Rings film. | |
| publisher | *Verlag, Verleger* | In the 1990s it was difficult for J. K. Rowling to find a publisher for her first Harry Potter book. | |
| quality paper | *seriöse Tageszeitung* | The "Daily Telegraph" is a British quality paper. | ≠ tabloid |
| regional | *regional* | Britain has a large number of regional papers. | ≠ national, nationwide |
| rehearsal<br>(to) rehearse | *Probe*<br>*proben* | Rehearsals for our new school play will start next week. | |
| remote control | *Fernbedienung* | The first TV remote control was sold in the 1950s. | |
| report<br>(to) report | *Bericht*<br>*berichten* | The World Health Organisation published a new report about the dangers of alcohol. | |
| review<br>(to) review | *Rezension, Kritik*<br>*kritisieren, überprüfen* | The group's latest CD received a positive review. | |
| sale<br>(to) sell | *Verkauf*<br>*verkaufen* | Sales of the new video game have gone up. | |

| vocabulary | dt. Bedeutung | English sentence | syn/opp |
|---|---|---|---|
| satellite TV | *Satelliten-fernsehen* | When you have satellite TV you can watch hundreds of TV programmes. | |
| screen | *Bildschirm* | My father bought a TV set with a bigger screen. | |
| series | *Serie* | "Star Trek" is one of the most popular TV series. | |
| slogan | *Werbespruch* | The first Coca Cola slogan was "The pause that refreshes". | |
| soap opera | *Familienserie* | The British TV soap opera "Coronation Street" was started in 1960. | |
| (to) sponsor<br>sponsor | *sponsern, finanziell unterstützen*<br>*Sponsor, Förderer* | Companies like Nike or Coca Cola sponsor sport events. | = (to) finance |
| (to) switch off | *ausschalten* | If you find the show too boring, switch off the TV. | = (to) turn off<br>≠ (to) switch on |
| tabloid | *Boulevardzeitung, Klatschzeitung* | The tabloids printed the latest news about the marriage of Brad Pitt. | ≠ quality paper |
| television set (TV set) | *Fernsehapparat* | Our neighbours are the only people I know who haven't got a television set. | |
| ticket | *Karte* | I couldn't get a ticket for the Coldplay concert in Glasgow. | |
| ticket sale | *Kartenverkauf* | The film *Harry Potter and the Sorcerer's Stone* broke every record for ticket sales. | |
| (to) tune in | *(ein Programm) einstellen, zuhören* | We hope you'll tune in again next week when we look at the latest films. | |

| vocabulary | dt. Bedeutung | English sentence | syn/opp |
| --- | --- | --- | --- |
| (to) turn down | *(Lautstärke) leiser stellen* | "Please turn your music down, Stewart." | |
| (to) turn off | *(Radio, Fernseher) ausschalten* | I was fed up with the silly programme, so I turned it off. | = (to) switch off |
| (to) turn on | *(Radio, Fernseher) an-, einschalten* | With a remote control you can turn on your TV set from where you are sitting. | = (to) switch on |
| TV commercial | *Fernsehspot* | TV commercials give information on products and services. | |
| variety<br>various | *Vielfalt*<br>*vielfältig, verschieden* | Today we can choose from a variety of TV channels. | |
| viewer | *(Fernseh-) Zuschauer* | The TV company hopes that the new series will attract more viewers. | |
| volume | *Lautstärke* | A little switch allows you to control the volume of the player. | |
| volume | *(Buch-) Band* | The Encyclopaedia Britannica has 35 volumes. | |
| (to) watch TV | *fernsehen* | How many hours a day do you watch TV? | |

# Technology

| vocabulary | dt. Bedeutung | English sentence | syn/opp |
|---|---|---|---|
| (to) advance<br>advance | *voranschreiten*<br>*Fortschritt* | In computer games you advance from one level to the next. | = (to) progress<br>= progress |
| answering machine | *Anrufbeantworter* | You can leave a message on an answering machine. | |
| artificial | *künstlich* | In 1957, the Soviets put the first artificial satellite into orbit. | ≠ natural |
| atomic energy | *Atomenergie* | Is atomic energy the answer to our energy problems? | = nuclear energy |
| (to) be in favour of | *für etwas sein; zugunsten* | Are you in favour of the use of nuclear power? | ≠ (to) be against |
| button | *Knopf* | "You push this button here to start the programme." | = key |
| at the push of a button | *auf Knopfdruck* | You can surf the Internet at the push of a button. | |
| (to) cancel (an action) | *(eine Aktion) abbrechen* | If you want to cancel the action, press the Escape-key. | |
| (to) cause damage | *Schaden verursachen* | Computer viruses cause millions of dollars of damage every year. | |
| CD | *CD (Compact Disk)* | a disk which contains music or computer data | |
| cell phone [AE] | *Handy, Mobiltelefon* | Cell phones are popular with teenagers. | = mobile phone [BE] |
| circle | *Kreis* | Strange circles appeared in cornfields over night. | |
| (to) circle | *umkreisen* | The spaceship circled the moon. | |

| vocabulary | dt. Bedeutung | English sentence | syn/opp |
|---|---|---|---|
| (to) click (on) a button | *auf eine Schaltfläche klicken* | Click this button to end the programme. | |
| clone, cloning | *Klon, Nachbau Schaffung von erbgleichen Wesen, Klonen* | Scottish scientists produced clones – artificial twins – of animals. | |
| commander<br>(to) command | *Befehlshaber*<br>*befehlen, gebieten* | James T. Kirk was made commander of the Starship Enterprise. | |
| complicated | *kompliziert* | My mother finds computers too complicated. | = difficult, complex |
| computer application | *Computeranwendung, Informatik* | Paul did a computer application course at his school. | |
| computer scientist | *Informatiker* | Computer scientists are working on the "thinking computer". | |
| (to) connect | *verbinden* | All of the PCs at our firm are connected to a central computer. | |
| connection | *Verbindung* | If you have a fast internet connection, you can download pictures quickly. | |
| contact | *Verbindung, Kontakt* | Mission Control in Houston lost contact with the Space Shuttle Columbia. | |
| (to) contact | *Verbindung aufnehmen* | Please contact us if you need help. | |
| crash helmet | *Sturzhelm* | All motorcyclists must wear crash helmets. | |
| (to) create | *schaffen, erschaffen* | The World Wide Web was created in the early 1990s. | |
| creation | *Erschaffung* | | |
| creature | *Geschöpf* | | |

| vocabulary | dt. Bedeutung | English sentence | syn/opp |
|---|---|---|---|
| (to) create | *ein Dokument erstellen* | I created my first document, using MS Word. | |
| crew | *Mannschaft* | All seven crew members of the space shuttle were killed in the accident. | = team |
| cure<br>(to) cure | *Heilung*<br>*heilen* | Will there ever be a cure for cancer? | = remedy, medication |
| current | *aktuell* | The current prices for flat rates are still too high. | = present |
| data | *Daten, Angaben* | Be careful when somebody asks you for your personal data on the Internet. | |
| data processing | *Datenverarbeitung* | Data processing is carried out by computers. | |
| (to) delete a document | *löschen* | Benjamin deleted the document which contained his essay by mistake. | |
| (to) design<br>design | *entwerfen, gestalten*<br>*Entwurf, Gestaltung* | Helen learnt to design a webpage. | |
| (to) discover<br>discovery | *entdecken*<br>*Entdeckung* | In 1492 Columbus discovered America. | |
| drive (in a computer) | *Laufwerk* | Today, all computers have a CD-ROM drive. | |
| (to) drive a car | *Auto fahren* | You have to pay to drive a car into central London. | |
| driving licence | *Führerschein* | My father has had his driving licence for more than thirty years. | |
| driving school | *Fahrschule* | Liz had a couple of lessons with the driving school before she took her test. | |
| driving test | *Fahrprüfung* | In Britain you can take your driving test at 17. | |

| vocabulary | dt. Bedeutung | English sentence | syn/opp |
|---|---|---|---|
| engine | *Motor* | Diesel engines are used for large vehicles. | = motor |
| engineer<br>(to) engineer | *Ingenieur, Konstrukteur*<br>*konstruieren, bauen* | In 1876 the German engineer Nicolaus August Otto built a new type of engine. | |
| engineering | *Ingenieurwesen, Maschinenbau* | (the study of) the work that is done by an engineer | |
| (to) enter<br><br><br>entrance<br>entry | *eingeben (Benutzernamen und Passwort);*<br>*eintreten*<br>*Eintritt, Zugang*<br>*Zutritt, Zugang* | Please enter your user name and password here.<br>Enter at your own risk. | |
| evolution<br>(to) evolve | *Evolution, Entwicklung*<br>*sich entwickeln* | In 1925 a biology teacher was not allowed to teach the theory of evolution at an American school. | |
| (to) execute (a command)<br>execution | *ausführen (einen Befehl)*<br>*Ausführung, Hinrichtung* | At a computer you execute a command with the Enter key. | |
| expert | *Fachmann* | Some of my classmates are real computer experts. | = specialist |
| (to) explore<br>exploration | *erforschen*<br>*Erforschung* | People have always dreamed of exploring outer space. | |
| (to) extend<br>extension<br>extensive | *ausweiten*<br>*Erweiterung*<br>*ausgedehnt, ausführlich* | Ebay wants to extend its business in China.<br>The extension of MS Word is *.doc. | |
| (to) fail a driving test | *bei einer Führerscheinprüfung durchfallen* | Poor old George failed his driving test twice. | ≠ (to) pass |

| vocabulary | dt. Bedeutung | English sentence | syn/opp |
|---|---|---|---|
| folder | *Verzeichnis; Ordner; Aktenordner* | I cannot remember in which folder I saved my essay. | = directory |
| (to) function | *funktionieren* | My new laptop computer functions perfectly. | = (to) work |
| gene | *Gen* | Gregor Mendel was one of the first people who studied genes. | |
| genetic engineering | *Gentechnik* | We hope that genetic engineering will help to cure illnesses. | |
| genetically modified food (GM food) | *gentechnisch veränderte Nahrungsmittel* | Many people think that genetically modified (GM) food is not good for us. | |
| global | *global, weltweit* | Global positioning systems (GPS) tell travellers where they are. | = worldwide |
| gravity | *Schwerkraft* | There is no gravity in outer space. | |
| (to) guide<br>guide<br><br>guidance | *führen, leiten*<br>*(Fremden-) Führer, Reiseleiter*<br>*Leitung, Führung* | A new technique was invented to guide and control a rocket. | |
| habitat | *Lebensraum* | the natural home or environment of an animal, plant, or other organism | = environment, surroundings |
| hard disk | *Festplatte* | My music files take up a lot of room on my hard disk. | = hard drive |
| (to) infect<br><br>infection | *infizieren, anstecken*<br>*Ansteckung* | A computer virus infected computers around the world. | |
| (to) inherit | *erben* | Some people inherit illnesses from their parents. | |
| inheritance | *Erbe* | Gregor Mendel discovered the laws of inheritance. | |

| vocabulary | dt. Bedeutung | English sentence | syn/opp |
|---|---|---|---|
| inherited disease | *Erbkrankheit* | Haemophilia ("Bluter-krankheit") is an inherited disease. | |
| (to) install | *aufstellen, installieren* | ENIAC, a computer in-stalled at the University of Pennsylvania in 1946, weighed about 30 tons. | = (to) set up<br>≠ (to) remove |
| (to) introduce<br>introduction | *einführen*<br>*Einführung, Einleitung* | Many firms introduce robots and computers in order to produce more cheaply. | |
| (to) invent<br>invention<br>inventor | *erfinden*<br>*Erfindung*<br>*Erfinder* | Coca Cola was invented in the 19th century (1886) by John S. Pemberton. | |
| isolated<br>(to) isolate<br>isolation | *einsam*<br>*isolieren*<br>*Isolation, Absonderung* | Do computer users become more isolated? | = lonely, lonesome |
| (to) keep in touch | *in Verbindung bleiben* | It is easy to keep in touch by sending e-mails. | ≠ (to) lose touch/contact |
| key | *Taste; Schlüssel* | Press any key to continue. | = button |
| keyboard | *Tastatur* | I bought myself a new keyboard. | |
| lane | *Spur* | In many cities there are special lanes for buses. | |
| (to) launch<br>launch | *(eine Rakete usw.) starten*<br>*Start* | In 1957 the Russians launched a satellite called Sputnik. | |
| level | *Niveau, Ebene* | Modern computer games are divided into several levels. | |
| (to) limit<br>limit<br>limitation | *begrenzen*<br>*Grenze*<br>*Begrenzung* | Several space missions brought only limited success. | |

| vocabulary | dt. Bedeutung | English sentence | syn/opp |
|---|---|---|---|
| (to) manage | *(etwas) fertig bringen* | The Russians managed to put a man into space. | |
| means<br>means of communication<br>means of transport | *Mittel*<br>*Kommunikationsmittel*<br>*Verkehrsmittel* | Young people like using the latest means of communication. | |
| message | *Nachricht, Botschaft* | "Please leave your message after the tone." | |
| mobile (phone) | *Handy, Mobiltelefon* | Text messages can be sent by computer or mobile phone. | = cellular phone, cell phone |
| (to) modify | *ändern* | A computer virus can modify programmes. | = (to) change |
| on the Internet | *im Internet* | It is easy to find information on the Internet. | = on the web |
| operating system<br>(to) operate | *Betriebssystem*<br>*funktionieren* | "Windows" is the world's No. 1 operating system for computers. | |
| orbit<br>(to) orbit | *Kreisbahn, Umlaufbahn*<br>*umkreisen* | The Russians put the first satellite into orbit around the Earth. | <br>= (to) circle |
| (to) overtake | *überholen* | Jamie tried to overtake the lorry. | |
| (to) pass a driving test | *Führescheinprüfung bestehen* | Julie passed her driving test after 23 driving lessons. | ≠ (to) fail |
| (to) paste | *einfügen;*<br>*kleben* | to copy or move text into a document from another text passage or another document<br>to paste wallpaper onto the walls | |
| (to) press a button | *eine Taste drücken* | Press this button to continue. | |

| vocabulary | dt. Bedeutung | English sentence | syn/opp |
|---|---|---|---|
| printer | *Drucker* | In our firm we have five printers. | |
| (to) process | *verarbeiten* | The computer processes a lot of information in seconds. | |
| (to) protect<br>protection | *schützen*<br>*Schutz* | In space astronauts must wear special clothing to protect themselves. | |
| race | *Wettlauf, Rennen* | In the 1950s the Americans and the Russians started the race into space. | |
| (to) receive<br>receiver<br>reception | *empfangen*<br>*Empfänger*<br>*Empfang* | Some mobile phones allow you to send and receive pictures. | |
| (to) recognize<br>recognition | *erkennen*<br>*(An-) Erkennung* | Some computers can recognize speech. | |
| (to) record | *aufzeichnen, aufnehmen* | With a VCR (videocassette recorder) you can record television programmes. | |
| (to) rely on | *sich verlassen auf* | Today, all industries rely on computers. | |
| (to) research<br>research<br>researcher | *forschen*<br>*Forschung*<br>*Forscher* | Scientists research to find cures for illnesses. | |
| (to) ride a bike | *Rad fahren* | In university towns many students ride bikes. | |
| ring tone | *Klingelton* | Young people spend a lot of money on ring tones. | |
| rocket | *Rakete* | The Saturn V rocket, which was used in the Apollo programme, was more than 110 metres tall. | |
| satellite | *Satellit* | Sputnik 1 was the first satellite in space. | |

| vocabulary | dt. Bedeutung | English sentence | syn/opp |
|---|---|---|---|
| (to) save | *sichern, speichern (eine Datei)* | Save all your English documents in the same folder. | |
| safe<br>safety | *sicher*<br>*Sicherheit* | The control centre was worried about the safety of the astronauts. | ≠ unsafe, dangerous |
| scientific<br>science | *wissenschaftlich*<br>*Naturwissenschaft* | The astronauts carried out scientific experiments. | |
| scientist | *Naturwissenschaftler* | Robert Koch was a famous German scientist. | |
| sea level | *Meeresebene* | Death Valley in California is lies 86 metres below sea level. | |
| search engine<br>(to) search | *Suchmaschine*<br>*suchen* | Google is the most the successful internet search engine. | |
| seat belt | *Sicherheitsgurt* | All drivers and passengers must wear seat belts. | |
| SMS | *(Abk.: Short Message Service) Kurznachricht* | Young people use SMS more often than e-mail. | |
| (to) solve<br>solution | *lösen; auflösen*<br>*Lösung* | We use computers to solve scientific and engineering problems. | |
| space, outer space | *Weltraum, Raum, Weltraum* | Would you like to fly into space? | |
| space exploration | *Erforschung des Weltraums* | The age of space exploration began in 1957 with the Russian satellite Sputnik 1. | |
| space suit | *Raumanzug* | The astronauts had to wear space suits when they left their spaceship. | |
| space travel | *Raumfahrt* | Space travel began in the1960s. | |

| vocabulary | dt. Bedeutung | English sentence | syn/opp |
|---|---|---|---|
| spaceship | *Raumschiff* | After landing their spaceship on the moon, the astronauts started their experiments. | |
| speed limit | *Geschwindigkeitsbegrenzung* | The speed limit in towns is 30 miles per hour. | |
| (to) store<br>storage | *speichern*<br>*Speicherung* | You can store more data on a DVD than on a CD. | = (to) save |
| surface | *Oberfläche* | The first man who walked on the surface of the moon was the American astronaut Neil Armstrong. | |
| technical<br><br>technique | *technisch, fachlich, Fach-*<br>*Technik* | These technical problems can only be solved by experts. | |
| technology | *Technologie* | In England, 14-year-olds have to take a test in information and communications technology. | |
| texting<br><br>(to) text | *Schreiben von SMS*<br>*eine SMS schreiben* | Young people prefer texting to writing letters. | |
| (to) trace | *aufspüren, ausfindig machen, finden* | You can trace friends and relatives on the web. | = (to) find |
| traffic | *Verkehr* | Big cities such as London have a lot of traffic problems. | |
| traffic jam | *Verkehrsstau* | There was a traffic jam on the road to the city centre. | = congestion |
| traffic sign | *Verkehrszeichen* | The Romans put up the first traffic signs. | |
| (to) transmit | *übertragen* | A telephone transmits sounds over electric wires. | |

| vocabulary | dt. Bedeutung | English sentence | syn/opp |
| --- | --- | --- | --- |
| treatment<br>(to) treat | *Behandlung*<br>*behandeln* | Mrs Walton broke her leg and was taken to hospital for treatment. | |
| (to) turn off (the computer) | *den Computer ausschalten* | For some kids it is very hard to turn off their computer. | = (to) switch off<br>≠ (to) switch on, (to) turn on |
| vehicle | *Fahrzeug* | No vehicles are allowed into the city centre between 8 a.m. and 6 p.m. | |
| virtual | *virtuell; nicht echt, nicht in Wirklichkeit vorhanden, nur im Internet* | An English website offers a virtual tour of Stonehenge. | |
| virus | *Virus* | Many computer viruses were written by teenagers. | = worm |
| wireless | *drahtlos* | Modern laptops can use a wireless connection to the Internet. | |
| workshop | *Werkstatt* | We have to send the broken machine to the workshop. | |

# Environment

| vocabulary | dt. Bedeutung | English sentence | syn/opp |
|---|---|---|---|
| acid rain | *saurer Regen* | Acid rain damages our forests, buildings and rivers. | |
| (to) affect | *betreffen, auf etwas einwirken* | A climate change will affect us all. | |
| alternative | *Alternative, andere Möglichkeit* | Wind energy is an alternative to atomic (nuclear) energy. | |
| atmosphere | *Atmosphäre* | The atmosphere protects the Earth like a warming blanket. | |
| aware<br>(to) be aware | *bewusst*<br>*bewusst sein* | People have become aware how important it is to protect the environment. | |
| balance | *Gleichgewicht* | The balance of nature has been disturbed. | |
| carbon dioxide | *Kohlendioxid* | The greenhouse effect is caused when too much carbon dioxide is released into the air. | |
| catastrophe | *Katastrophe* | The Florida hurricane was a catastrophe that destroyed many houses. | = disaster |
| climate | *Klima* | Poorer, developing countries will suffer more from climate change than wealthy ones. | |
| climate change | *Klimawandel* | | |
| (to) consume<br>consumer<br>consumption | *verbrauchen*<br>*Verbraucher*<br>*Verbrauch* | We should try to consume less. | |

| vocabulary | dt. Bedeutung | English sentence | syn/opp |
|---|---|---|---|
| (to) contaminate | *verseuchen* | Many rivers and lakes were contaminated with chemicals. | = (to) pollute |
| contamination | *Verunreinigung, Verseuchung* | | |
| creature | *Lebewesen* | People believe that a strange creature lives in the lake of Loch Ness. | |
| (to) create | *(er)schaffen* | | |
| (to) depend on | *abhängen von, abhängig sein von* | The industrialized countries depend on oil. | |
| dependent | *abhängig* | | ≠ independent |
| dependency, dependence | *Abhängigkeit* | | ≠ independence |
| (to) destroy | *zerstören* | Since the 1940s, about half the world's rainforests have been destroyed. | |
| destruction | *Zerstörung* | The singer Sting says "Stop the destruction of the rainforests!" | |
| destructive | *zerstörerisch* | | |
| detergent | *Reingungsmittel* | Household detergents pollute our rivers. | |
| developed countries | *Industriestaaten, Industrieländer* | The developed countries are producing too much waste. | = industrialized countries ≠ developing countries, Third World countries |
| (to) die out | *aussterben* | More rare animals are about to die out. | = (to) become extinct |
| (to) disappear | *verschwinden* | Dinosaurs have long disappeared from the Earth. | |
| disappearance | *Verschwinden* | | |
| disaster | *Unglück, Katastrophe* | The recent oil tanker accident was a disaster for the Spanish coastal towns. | = catastrophe |

| vocabulary | dt. Bedeutung | English sentence | syn/opp |
| --- | --- | --- | --- |
| disposable bottle | *Einwegflasche* | a bottle which is not returned to the shop | ≠ return bottle |
| disposal | *Beseitigung, Entsorgung* | There are special containers for the disposal of nuclear waste. | |
| drought | *Dürre* | a long period of dry weather without any rain | ≠ flood |
| (to) dry up | *austrocknen, vertrockenen* | Because of the long drought many rivers have dried up. | |
| dump | *Müllhalde* | We should not use the oceans as cheap dumps. | |
| (to) dump | *abladen, ablagern* | Old car tyres have been dumped into the river. | |
| dumping ground | *Müllhalde, -kippe* | Some nations use the oceans as dumping ground for chemical waste. | |
| earthquake | *Erdbeben* | The San Francisco Earthquake of 1906 killed 3,000 people and destroyed 28,000 buildings. | |
| effect | *Wirkung, Auswirkung* | What will be the effects of changing temperatures on plants and animals? | = consequence |
| (to) effect | *bewirken* | | |
| effective | *wirkungsvoll* | | |
| energy conservation | *Energieeinsparung* | Most Americans are not interested in energy conservation. | |
| energy consumption | *Energieverbrauch* | The developed countries should reduce their energy consumption. | |
| energy source | *Energiequelle* | Wind and solar energy are alternative sources of energy. | |
| environment | *Umwelt* | the natural world in which people, animals and plants live | = surroundings |

| vocabulary | dt. Bedeutung | English sentence | syn/opp |
|---|---|---|---|
| environmental studies | *Umweltforschung* | Environmental studies show us how we can save our planet. | |
| environmentalist | *Umweltschützer* | Environmentalists worry about the fast disappearance of the rainforest. | = conservationist |
| environmentally aware | *umweltbewusst* | The number of environmentally aware young people is increasing. | |
| environmentally friendly | *umweltfreundlich* | When shopping I make sure that the product I buy is environmentally friendly. | |
| evolution<br>(to) evolve | *Entwicklung (Evolution)*<br>*sich entwickeln* | Charles Darwin developed the theory of "evolution by natural selection". | |
| (to) forbid | *verbieten* | It is forbidden to throw rubbish into a river. | ≠ (to) permit, (to) allow |
| fossil fuel | *fossiler Brennstoff* | Coal, petroleum, and natural gas are examples of fossil fuel. | |
| global warming | *Erwärmung der Erde, Erderwärmung* | People have become more aware of the danger of global warming. | |
| greenhouse effect | *Treibhauseffekt* | the warming of the Earth's surface | |
| greenhouse gases | *Treibhausgase* | Cars and refrigerators produce greenhouse gases. | |
| hygiene | *Hygiene* | Hygiene standards in Third World countries are low. | |
| industrial waste | *Industrieabfall* | Until recently, some countries threw their industrial waste into the sea. | |
| junk | *Müll, Abfall* | Ed's room is filled with junk. | = trash, litter, refuse, waste |

| vocabulary | dt. Bedeutung | English sentence | syn/opp |
|---|---|---|---|
| (to) load<br>load | *belasten*<br>*Last* | We have loaded our air with dangerous chemicals. | = burden |
| marine life | *Meeresfauna, Meeresflora* | plants and animals of the sea | |
| natural gas | *Erdgas* | Natural gas was found on some Indian reservations. | |
| nuclear power plant | *Atomkraftwerk* | In 1986 a Soviet nuclear power plant at Chernobyl exploded. | = nuclear/ atomic power station |
| nuclear waste | *Atommüll* | We need a safe place for nuclear waste. | |
| oil slick | *Ölteppich* | A large oil slick appeared after the tanker had hit a rock. | |
| overpopulation | *Überbevölkerung* | too many people living in one place | |
| ozone layer | *Ozonschicht* | People are worried about holes in the ozone layer. | |
| (to) persuade | *jmdn. überzeugen (etwas zu tun)* | We must persuade people to use paper bags instead of plastic ones. | |
| pesticide | *Schädlingsbekämpfungsmittel* | Farmers use fertilizers to kill insects and diseases. | |
| petrol [BE] | *Benzin* | Big cars use too much petrol. | = gas [AE] |
| petroleum | *Rohöl* | OPEC is short for "Organisation of Petroleum Exporting Countries". | |
| poisonous<br>poison | *giftig*<br>*Gift, Schadstoff* | Fish in the sea were killed by petrol and poisonous chemicals. | = toxic |

| vocabulary | dt. Bedeutung | English sentence | syn/opp |
| --- | --- | --- | --- |
| polar ice caps | *Polkappen* | Two per cent of the Earth's water is locked up as ice in glaciers ("Gletscher") and the polar ice caps. | |
| (to) pollute | *verschmutzen* | Automobiles and smoke from factories pollute the air. | = (to) contaminate |
| polluting | *umweltschädlich* | We should use less polluting forms of power, such as solar energy. | |
| pollution | *Verschmutzung* | In the 1950s and 1960s, nobody thought about pollution. | |
| power station | *Kraftwerk* | A fire broke out at the Russian power station at Chernobyl. | = power plant |
| (to) protect<br>protection | *schützen*<br>*Schutz* | A group of US and Japanese scientists wants to protect apes and rhinos. | = (to) guard, (to) safeguard |
| rain forest | *Regenwald* | Tropical rain forests cover 7 % of the Earth's surface. | |
| raw material | *Rohstoff* | We mustn't waste our raw materials. | = resources |
| (to) recycle | *recyceln, wieder aufbereiten* | In many shops they use recycled paper. | |
| recycling | *Wiederverwertung* | Recycling firms help to save raw materials. | |
| (to) reduce<br>reduction | *verringern*<br>*Verringerung* | We must try to reduce the amount of waste. | |
| (to) release | *freisetzen, freilassen* | When coal and petroleum are burned, they release dangerous gases into the air. | = (to) set free |
| renewable | *erneuerbar* | Wind power is a renewable source of energy. | |

| vocabulary | dt. Bedeutung | English sentence | syn/opp |
|---|---|---|---|
| (to) repair | *reparieren* | Meat and fish provide protein, which helps our bodies to grow and repair themselves. | |
| resources | *Bodenschätze, Ressourcen, Mittel* | Coal, oil and wood are natural resources. | = raw materials |
| return bottle | *Mehrwegflasche* | a bottle which you return to the shop so that it can be used again | ≠ disposable bottle |
| reusable | *wieder verwertbar* | Reusable packaging could help solve our waste problem. | |
| (to) reuse | *wieder verwenden* | Don't throw this plastic bag away – reuse it! | |
| (to) save | *sparen; retten* | Think about how you could save electricity.<br>Help save our planet! | |
| scientist | *Wissenschaftler* | Scientists study the effects of climate change. | |
| skin cancer | *Hautkrebs* | If you often stay in the sun for too long, you can develop skin cancer. | |
| solar energy | *Sonnenenergie* | In the future, men will make use of solar energy. | |
| solar system | *Sonnensystem* | The Earth is different from all the other planets in our solar system. | |
| source | *Quelle* | | |
| source of energy | *Energiequelle* | Nuclear power is a clean but dangerous source of energy. | |
| species | *Art* | Thousands of species could die out because of global warming. | |

| vocabulary | dt. Bedeutung | English sentence | syn/opp |
|---|---|---|---|
| surface | *Oberfläche* | It is quite possible that the surface of the Earth will warm by about another 3,5 degrees over the next century. | |
| survival<br>(to) survive | *Überleben*<br>*überleben* | Animals in mountain areas have better chances of survival. | |
| threat | *Bedrohung* | Poisonous chemicals are a threat to our oceans. | = menace, hazard, risk |
| (to) threaten | *bedrohen* | The coastal cities were threatened by flooding. | = (to) endanger |
| toxic waste | *Giftmüll* | Where shall we put our toxic waste? | = poisonous rubbish |
| village | *Dorf* | Terry lives with his parents and his younger sister in a quiet village. | |
| waste | *Abfall* | Some big firms have not done much about waste yet. | = junk, litter, rubbish, refuse |
| (to) waste | *vergeuden* | Do not waste your talents. | |
| waste paper | *Altpapier* | Waste paper is a valuable raw material. | |
| waste separation | *Mülltrennung* | Germans are good at waste separation. | |
| waste water | *Abwasser* | Waste water must not flow into our rivers. | = sewage |
| wind energy | *Windenergie* | We need more wind energy when oil runs out. | |
| wind farm, wind park | *Windpark* | Some people say that wind farms spoil the landscape. | |

# Politics and Institutions

| vocabulary | dt. Bedeutung | English sentence | syn/opp |
|---|---|---|---|
| agreement | *Übereinkunft, Vereinbarung, Vertrag* | After long discussions we came to an agreement. | ≠ disagreement |
| (to) agree | *übereinstimmen, zustimmen* | | |
| (to) argue | *sich (mit jmdm. über/wegen etwas) streiten, zanken* | Daniel and Josh are always arguing about their political views. | = (to) quarrel, (to) fight |
| (to) arrest | *festnehmen, verhaften* | A 25-year-old man was arrested because he had shot John Lennon. | ≠ (to) set free, (to) release |
| armed forces | *Streitkräfte* | The president sent more armed forces to fight in Iraq. | = military forces, soldiers |
| attitude | *Haltung, Einstellung* | Party members often have different attitudes. | = view, opinion |
| bill | *Gesetzentwurf* | The Senate discussed a new education bill. | = law |
| campaign | *Werbefeldzug, Wahlkampf* | The president started a campaign for his re-election. | |
| (to) cast (a vote) | *abstimmen* | When you are 18 you can cast your vote for the first time. | = (to) vote |
| ceremony | *Feier, Zeremonie* | In a ceremony in Tucson more than 1,000 people became US citizens. | |
| challenge<br>challenger<br>(to) challenge | *Herausforderung*<br>*Herausforderer*<br>*herausfordern* | The fight against poverty is a great challenge for the government. | <br>= rival, competitor |

| vocabulary | dt. Bedeutung | English sentence | syn/opp |
|---|---|---|---|
| charity | *wohltätige Zwecke* *Wohltätigkeit (-sorganisation)* | The millionaire gave all his money to charity. The Red Cross is a charity organization. | |
| citizen | *Staatsbürger* | Andy Garcia was born on the Island of Cuba, but he is an American citizen. | |
| city council | *Stadtrat* | The city council decided to pull down old houses in the centre. | |
| commission | *Kommission, Ausschuss* | A commission will look into the problems of young unmarried mothers. | |
| committee | *Ausschuss* | A committee will work out the programme for the open day at our school. | |
| Congress [AE] | *Kongress* | The US Congress meets in the Capitol in Washington. | |
| (to) conquer | *erobern* | In 1066 William of Normandy conquered England. | |
| conquest | *Eroberung* | We talked about the Norman conquest. | |
| constitution | *Verfassung* | Great Britain does not have a written constitution. Germany has one, it is called "Grundgesetz". | = fundamental law |
| council flat | *Sozialwohnung* | The government gives teenage mothers a free council flat if they go back to school. | |
| court | *Gericht* | You must tell the truth in court. | |
| death penalty | *Todesstrafe* | Many people are against the death penalty. | = capital punishment |

| vocabulary | dt. Bedeutung | English sentence | syn/opp |
|---|---|---|---|
| declaration<br>(to) declare | *Erklärung*<br>*(to) declare* | President Wilson asked the US Congress for a declaration of war in 1917. | |
| Declaration of Independence | *Unabhängigkeitserklärung* | The Declaration of Independence was written by the thirteen American colonies in 1776. | |
| (to) demonstrate<br>demonstration | *demonstrieren*<br>*Demonstration* | Blacks and whites demonstrated against the war in Iraq. | |
| department | *Ministerium, Abteilung* | Muriel Reed works as a secretary in the department of defence ("Verteidigungsministerium"). | |
| district | *Gebiet, Bezirk* | Brixton is a district in South London where many black people live. | |
| duty | *Dienst, Pflicht* | Police officer Jones is on night duty this week. | |
| election<br>(to) elect | *Wahl*<br>*wählen* | In Germany, there is an election to the Bundestag every four years. | |
| emergency | *Notfall* | In case of an emergency please pull this chain! | |
| European Union | *Europäische Union* | What do you know about the history of the European Union (EU)? | |
| (to) execute<br>execution | *hinrichten*<br>*Hinrichtung* | Texas executed 23 criminals in the year 2004. | |
| extract | *Auszug* | The students had to learn an extract from the Declaration of Independence. | = excerpt, passage |

| vocabulary | dt. Bedeutung | English sentence | syn/opp |
|---|---|---|---|
| government<br>(to) govern | *Regierung*<br>*regieren* | The government must help people who cannot find work. | |
| head of state | *Staatsoberhaupt* | The US president is head of state and also head of the government. | |
| independent<br>independence | *unabhängig*<br>*Unabhängigkeit* | The American colonies wanted to be independent. | ≠ dependent<br>≠ dependence |
| involved<br>(to) become/ get involved | *beteiligt sein an, etwas zu tun haben mit* | Mary and Harry are involved in the politics in their hometown. | |
| issue | *Streitfrage* | Crime and drugs are important issues today. | = problem |
| (to) join | *beitreten, mitmachen* | Would you like to join a political party? | |
| law | *Gesetz* | The government passed a new law which helps working mothers. | |
| lawyer | *Rechtsanwalt* | I'll have to ask my lawyer before I say anything more. | |
| (to) make a difference | *etwas bewirken* | It does make a difference whether you go to an election or not. | |
| (to) make a speech | *eine Rede halten* | After her arrival at Philadelphia airport the Queen made a speech. | |
| mayor | *Bürgermeister* | The mayor will visit our youth club next Saturday. | |
| Member of Parliament | *Parlamentsabgeordneter* | In Britain there are more than 600 Members of Parliament. | |
| minister | *Minister* | The German environment minister said, "We have to reduce pollution." | |

| vocabulary | dt. Bedeutung | English sentence | syn/opp |
|---|---|---|---|
| monarchy | *Monarchie* | Most Britons want to keep the monarchy. | ≠ republic |
| nationality | *Nationalität* | Marc has double nationality: he has a German and a British passport. | |
| (to) nominate<br>nomination | *jmdn. nominieren*<br>*Ernennung* | The students nominated a girl and two boys for the position of class spokesman ("Klassensprecher"). | |
| (to) overwhelm<br>overwhelming | *überwältigen*<br>*überwältigend* | The Conservatives won an overwhelming majority. | |
| (to) pass a law | *ein Gesetz verabschieden* | Congress passed a new law on immigration. | |
| platform | *Parteiprogramm, Wahlplattform* | The Democratic Party worked out a new platform for the coming election. | = programme |
| platform | *Bahnsteig* | The next train for Welling leaves from platform 2. | |
| policy | *Politik, Taktik* | I do not agree with the government's housing policy. | |
| politician | *Politiker/in* | Film star Arnold Schwarzenegger decided to become a politician. | |
| politics<br>political | *Politik, Staatskunst*<br>*politisch* | Are you interested in politics? | |
| power | *Macht, Gewalt* | Tony Blair's Labour Party came to power in 1997. | |
| president<br>(to) preside | *Präsident*<br>*den Vorsitz haben* | The US president is head of the government and head of state. | |
| presidential | *Präsidenten-, Präsidentschafts-* | In the USA presidential elections are held every four years. | |

| vocabulary | dt. Bedeutung | English sentence | syn/opp |
|---|---|---|---|
| previous | *vorherig, vorhergehend* | The prime minister blamed the previous government for the bad economic situation of the country. | = former |
| prime minister | *Premierminister* | Margaret Thatcher (1979–1990) was Britain's first woman Prime Minister. | |
| process | *Prozess, Verfahren, Vorgang* | The peace process has come to a standstill. | |
| public | *Öffentlichkeit; öffentlich* | The general public is against higher taxes. | ≠ private |
| regulation | *Vorschrift* | There are no government regulations about religious services at school. | |
| (to) represent<br>representative | *vertreten*<br>*Vertreter* | The president represents our country abroad. | |
| resident<br><br>(to) reside | *Bewohner/in, Einwohner/in*<br>*wohnen* | My friend Shail's father comes from Bombay (Mumbai). He has been a resident in Britain for 25 years. | |
| right to vote | *Stimmrecht* | In many states, blacks did not have the right to vote. | = suffrage, franchise |
| royal | *königlich* | People all over the world are interested in the latest news about the British royal family. | |
| (to) run for (president) | *kandidieren (für das Präsidentenamt)* | In 1991 William Jefferson Clinton decided to run for president. | |
| Senate | *Senat* | There are 100 senators in the US Senate. | |
| session | *Sitzung, Sitzungsperiode* | The prime minister opened the session of the European Council in Cardiff. | = meeting, conference |

| vocabulary | dt. Bedeutung | English sentence | syn/opp |
|---|---|---|---|
| society<br>social | *Gesellschaft*<br>*gesellschaftlich* | There are too many poor people in our modern society. | |
| society | *Verein* | Ken and I joined the Historical Society of our city. | |
| suburb | *Vorort, Stadtrandsiedlung* | Most people prefer living in a suburb to living in the noisy city centre. | ≠ city centre, downtown |
| Supreme Court [AE] | *das Oberste Gericht* | The offices of the US Supreme Court are in Washington, D.C. | |
| tax | *Steuer* | There is a high tax on petrol and tobacco. | |
| term (of office) | *Amtszeit* | In November 2004 President George W. Bush was elected for a second term of office. | |
| town hall | *Rathaus* | The sportsmen who had won an Olympic medal were invited to a celebration in the town hall. | |
| trial | *Prozess* | The trial against Charles Evington took place in the Old Bailey in London. | |
| (to) vote | *abstimmen*<br>*Abstimmung* | When you are 18 you have the right to vote. | |

# Grundwortschatz

| | |
|---|---|
| a couple of | *ein paar* |
| a few | *einige* |
| (to) abandon | *aufgeben, preisgeben, verlassen* |
| abbreviation | *Abkürzung* |
| able | *fähig* |
| above | *über* |
| abroad | *ins, im Ausland* |
| (to) accept | *annehmen* |
| acceptable | *annehmbar* |
| accident | *Unfall* |
| according to | *entsprechend, gemäß* |
| acid rain | *saurer Regen* |
| (to) act | *handeln* |
| activity | *Tätigkeit* |
| actor | *Schauspieler* |
| actress | *Schauspielerin* |
| actual | *tatsächlich* |
| (to) add | *hinzufügen; zusammenzählen* |
| (to) address | *ansprechen* |
| address | *Adresse* |
| (to) admire | *bewundern* |
| admission | *Eintritt* |
| (to) admit | *zugeben, zugestehen* |
| (to) adopt | *adoptieren* |
| adult | *Erwachsener* |
| (to) advance | *vorrücken* |
| advantage (over) | *Vorteil (gegenüber)* |
| adventure | *Abenteuer* |
| advert | *Anzeige, Annonce* |
| advertisement | *(Zeitungs-) Anzeige* |
| advertising | *Werbung, Reklame* |
| advice | *Rat(schlag)* |
| aerobics | *Aerobic* |
| (to) affect | *sich auswirken auf, betreffen; (Gesundheit) angreifen* |
| (to) afford | *sich leisten (können)* |
| afraid | *verängstigt* |
| afternoon | *Nachmittag* |
| afterwards | *danach* |
| against | *gegen* |
| age | *Alter* |
| agent | *(Stell-) Vertreter* |
| (to) agree | *zustimmen, übereinstimmen* |

| | |
|---|---|
| agreement | *Vereinbarung* |
| ahead | *vorn, in Führung* |
| (to) aim | *zielen* |
| air | *Luft* |
| airport | *Flughafen* |
| alcohol | *Alkohol* |
| alive | *lebendig (noch am Leben)* |
| (to) allow | *erlauben* |
| almost | *fast, beinah* |
| alone | *allein* |
| alternative | *Ersatz-* |
| although | *obwohl, obgleich* |
| amazing | *erstaunlich* |
| ambulance | *Krankenwagen* |
| amount | *Menge, Betrag* |
| amusement | *Unterhaltung, Entzücken* |
| ancestor | *Vorfahr* |
| angel | *Engel* |
| anger | *Zorn, Ärger, Wut* |
| angry | *zornig* |
| (to) announce | *ankündigen, bekannt geben* |
| announcement | *Bekanntmachung* |
| (to) annoy | *ärgern, belästigen* |
| annual | *jährlich, Jahres …* |
| anonymous | *anonym* |
| apart | *getrennt, für sich* |
| (to) appeal | *gefallen; Berufung einlegen, appellieren* |
| (to) appear | *erscheinen* |
| appearance | *Erscheinen, Aufkommen* |
| application | *Bewerbung* |
| (to) apply for | *sich bewerben um* |
| apprentice | *Auszubildende(r)* |
| (to) approach | *sich nähern* |
| area | *Gebiet, Bereich* |
| (to) argue | *streiten, erörtern, diskutieren* |
| argument | *Wortwechsel* |
| (to) arrange | *verabreden, vereinbaren* |
| (to) arrest | *festnehmen, verhaften* |
| (to) arrive | *ankommen* |
| arrow | *Pfeil* |
| article | *Artikel* |
| artificial | *künstlich, Kunst-* |
| ashamed | *beschämt* |
| (to) ask for | *bitten* |
| aspect | *Gesichtspunkt* |
| assembly | *Aula; Versammlung* |

| | |
|---|---|
| assistant | *Assistent* |
| association | *Verband* |
| (to) assume | *glauben, annehmen* |
| at least | *wenigstens* |
| athletics | *Leichtathletik* |
| attack | *Angriff* |
| attempt | *Versuch* |
| (to) attend | *anwesend sein* |
| attention | *Aufmerksamkeit* |
| attitude | *Haltung, Einstellung* |
| (to) attract | *anziehen* |
| audience | *Publikum* |
| aunt | *Tante* |
| automatic | *automatisch* |
| autumn | *Herbst* |
| available | *erhältlich, verfügbar* |
| average | *Durchschnitt* |
| (to) avoid | *vermeiden* |
| award | *Preis* |
| aware | *bewusst* |
| awful | *schrecklich* |
| background | *Hintergrund* |
| baggage | *Gepäck [AE]* |
| balance | *Gleichgewicht* |
| bar chart | *Balkendiagramm* |
| barbecue | *Grillparty* |
| barely | *kaum* |
| (to) bark | *bellen* |
| bark | *Borke, Rinde* |
| basement | *Untergeschoss* |
| basic | *grundlegend, fundamental* |
| battery | *Batterie* |
| battle | *Schlacht* |
| bay | *(Meeres-) Bucht* |
| beach | *Strand* |
| (to) bear | *tragen* |
| because of | *wegen* |
| bedroom | *Schlafzimmer* |
| beef | *Rindfleisch* |
| (to) behave | *sich benehmen* |
| behaviour | *Verhalten, Benehmen* |
| behind | *hinten, dahinter, zurück* |
| belief | *Glaube, Überzeugung* |
| believable | *glaubwürdig, glaubhaft* |
| (to) believe in | *glauben an* |
| (to) belong | *gehören (zu), angehören* |
| below | *unten, unter* |
| belt | *Gürtel* |

| | |
|---|---|
| bench | *Bank, Sitzbank* |
| benefit | *Nutzen, Vorteil* |
| beside | *neben* |
| besides | *außer* |
| (to) besiege | *belagern* |
| (to) bet | *wetten* |
| beyond | *jenseits, darüber hinaus* |
| bicycle | *Fahrrad* |
| bilingual | *zweisprachig* |
| bill | *Rechnung* |
| bin | *Mülleimer* |
| biro | *Kugelschreiber* |
| (to) blame | *die Schuld geben* |
| blanket | *Decke, Wolldecke* |
| (to) bleed | *bluten, zur Ader lassen* |
| block of flats | *Wohnhaus, Mietshaus* |
| (to) blush | *erröten, rot werden* |
| board | *Brett* |
| boarding school | *Internat* |
| (to) boil | *kochen, abkochen* |
| bold | *kühn* |
| bolt | *Bolzen, Riegel, Schraube* |
| bookshelf | *Bücherregal* |
| boot | *(Auto) Kofferraum; Stiefel* |
| booth | *Kabine* |
| border | *Grenze* |
| bored | *gelangweilt* |
| boring | *langweilig* |
| (to) borrow | *borgen, sich ausleihen* |
| bottom | *Grund, unterster Teil, Boden* |
| bounty | *Belohnung* |
| bowl | *Schale, Schüssel, Napf* |
| box office | *Kasse* |
| bracket | *Klammer* |
| brain | *Gehirn, Verstand, Intelligenz* |
| (to) brake | *bremsen* |
| brave | *tapfer* |
| break | *Pause* |
| (to) break up | *sich trennen* |
| breath | *Atem* |
| (to) breathe | *atmen* |
| brick | *Ziegel* |
| brief | *kurz, bündig* |
| briefing | *(Einsatz-) Besprechung* |
| bright | *hell* |
| (to) bring up | *aufziehen, großziehen* |

| | |
|---|---|
| Briton | der Brite, die Britin |
| brochure | Broschüre |
| (to) brush | bürsten, putzen |
| (to) bully | schikanieren |
| bully | Rüpel |
| burden | Last |
| (to) burn | brennen, verbrennen |
| bus pass | Busfahrschein |
| business | Geschäft |
| busy | belebt, geschäftig |
| button | Knopf |
| by birth | von Geburt |
| by mistake | aus Versehen |
| by trade | von Beruf |
| cable | Tau, Kabel |
| cafeteria | Kantine, Selbstbedienungsrestaurant |
| cage | Käfig |
| cake | Kuchen |
| calendar | Kalender |
| (to) calm | beruhigen |
| (to) camp | zelten |
| campaign | Feldzug, Wahlkampf |
| camp-site | zelten |
| can | Dose |
| (to) cancel | (Termin, Zug, Auftrag) streichen, abbestellen, stornieren |
| cancer | Krebs |
| candidate | Kandidat |
| candle | Kerze |
| canteen | Kantine |
| cap | Mütze |
| capital | Hauptstadt |
| (to) capture | erobern |
| care | Sorgfalt |
| career | (berufliche) Laufbahn |
| carpenter | Zimmermann |
| carpet | Teppich |
| carriage | Wagen, (Zug-) Waggon |
| cartoon | Karikatur |
| case | Fall; Koffer |
| cash | Bargeld |
| (to) cast | werfen |
| category | Kategorie |
| cattle | Vieh |
| cause | Grund, Anlass |
| (to) cause | verursachen |
| central heating | Zentralheizung |
| centre | Mitte, Zentrum |

| | |
|---|---|
| century | *Jahrhundert* |
| cereal | *Getreide, Frühstücks-cerealien (Müsli)* |
| certain | *gewiss* |
| certainly | *sicherlich, bestimmt, gewiss* |
| chain | *Kette* |
| challenge | *Herausforderung* |
| champion | *Sieger(in), Champion* |
| championship | *Meisterschaft* |
| chance | *Möglichkeit, Gelegenheit* |
| change | *Wechselgeld* |
| (to) change | *sich verändern; wechseln* |
| channel | *(Fernseh-) Kanal, Programm* |
| (to) charge | *(Geld) verlangen, berechnen; angreifen* |
| charge | *Anklage* |
| charity | *Wohltätigkeit; Güte, Nachsicht* |
| chase | *Verfolgungsjagd* |
| (to) chat | *schwätzen* |
| cheap | *billig, preiswert* |
| (to) cheat | *betrügen, schummeln* |
| (to) check | *kontrollieren* |
| cheek | *Backe, Wange* |
| (to) cheer | *anfeuern* |
| chemical | *Chemikalie* |
| chemistry | *Chemie* |
| chess | *Schach* |
| chief | *oberster, wichtigster, Haupt-* |
| childhood | *Kindheit* |
| chill | *Frost, Kälte* |
| chips | *Pommes frites* |
| choice | *(Aus-) Wahl* |
| Christian | *Christ(in)* |
| citizen | *(Staats-) Bürger* |
| (to) claim | *beanspruchen, behaupten* |
| classical | *klassisch* |
| cleaner | *Reinigungspersonal* |
| clerk | *Angestellter* |
| cliff | *Klippe* |
| (to) climb | *klettern* |
| cloakroom | *Garderobe* |
| (to) close | *schließen* |
| close | *nahe; eng* |
| close to | *nahe bei* |
| cloth | *Tuch* |
| clue | *Lösungshilfe, Frage* |
| (to) collect | *versammeln* |

| | |
|---|---|
| column | *(Zeitungs-) Spalte* |
| (to) combine | *verbinden* |
| (to) come to terms | *sich einigen* |
| comfort | *Trost* |
| comfortable | *bequem* |
| commercial | *Werbespot* |
| (to) commit | *begehen* |
| committee | *Ausschuss* |
| common | *üblich, gewöhnlich* |
| common sense | *gesunder Menschenverstand* |
| commuter | *Pendler* |
| company | *Umgang, Gesellschaft; Firma, Betrieb* |
| (to) compare | *vergleichen* |
| (to) compete | *konkurrieren* |
| (to) complain | *sich beschweren* |
| (to) complete | *vollständig* |
| complicated | *kompliziert* |
| comprehensive school | *Gesamtschule* |
| concerned | *besorgt, betroffen* |
| concrete | *Beton* |
| confidence | *(Selbst-) Vertrauen* |
| confident | *zuversichtlich, selbstbewusst* |
| (to) connect | *verbinden* |
| (to) conquer | *erobern* |
| (to) consider | *betrachten, erwägen* |
| (to) consist (of) | *bestehen aus* |
| (to) consult | *um Rat fragen* |
| (to) consume | *verbrauchen* |
| (to) contain | *enthalten* |
| (to) continue | *fortfahren, weitermachen* |
| control | *Kontrolle* |
| convenient | *bequem, günstig* |
| conversation | *Gespräch* |
| (to) cooperate | *kooperieren* |
| (to) cough | *husten* |
| counter | *Ladentisch, Theke, Schalter* |
| county | *Grafschaft* |
| courage | *Mut* |
| course | *Kurs, Lehrgang* |
| court | *Gericht* |
| courtyard | *Hof* |
| crack | *Riss, Spalte* |
| (to) crash | *abstürzen* |
| (to) create | *(er)schaffen, schöpfen* |
| crime | *Verbrechen* |
| criminal | *Verbrecher* |

| | |
|---|---|
| criminal | *kriminell* |
| critic | *Kritiker* |
| criticism | *Kritik* |
| (to) criticize | *kritisieren* |
| crossing | *Überfahrt* |
| crowd | *Menge* |
| cruel | *grausam* |
| cupboard | *Schrank* |
| curious | *neugierig* |
| current | *gegenwärtig, aktuell* |
| curriculum vitae (CV) | *Lebenslauf* |
| customer | *Kunde, Kundin* |
| cut | *Schnittwunde* |
| (to) cut | *(Rasen) mähen, schneiden* |
| damage | *Schaden* |
| danger | *Gefahr* |
| date | *Verabredung* |
| (to) dawn | *dämmern, tagen* |
| (to) deal | *austeilen, handeln* |
| death penalty | *Todesstrafe* |
| debt | *Schulden* |
| decent | *anständig* |
| (to) decide | *sich entschließen, entscheiden* |
| decision | *Entscheidung* |
| declaration | *Erklärung* |
| (to) declare | *(öffentlich) erklären* |
| (to) decrease | *verringern* |
| defeat | *Niederlage* |
| defence | *Verteidigung* |
| (to) defend | *verteidigen* |
| definitely | *bestimmt* |
| degree | *Grad* |
| (to) delay | *Verspätung* |
| deliberate | *wohlüberlegt, vorsätzlich* |
| delight | *Vergnügen* |
| demand | *Nachfrage* |
| (to) deny | *abstreiten, bestreiten, leugnen* |
| (to) depart | *abfahren, fortgehen* |
| (to) depend (on, upon) | *abhängen, abhängig sein (von)* |
| (to) describe | *beschreiben* |
| description | *Beschreibung* |
| desert | *Wüste* |
| (to) design | *entwerfen; Entwurf* |
| desire | *Wunsch* |
| desperate | *verzweifelt* |
| (to) destroy | *zerstören* |

| | |
|---|---|
| (to) develop | *sich entwickeln* |
| diary | *Tagebuch* |
| dictionary | *Wörterbuch* |
| diet | *Kost, Nahrung* |
| (to) differ | *sich unterscheiden* |
| difference | *Unterschied* |
| different | *verschieden* |
| (to) dig | *graben* |
| (to) direct | *richten* |
| dirt | *Schmutz* |
| disadvantage | *Nachteil* |
| (to) disagree | *nicht zustimmen* |
| (to) disappear | *verschwinden* |
| (to) disappoint | *enttäuschen* |
| disaster | *(großes) Unglück* |
| (to) discover | *entdecken* |
| disease | *Krankheit* |
| dishes | *Geschirr (Plural)* |
| (to) dislike | *nicht mögen* |
| display | *(Schaufenster-) Auslage* |
| distance | *Entfernung* |
| (to) distract | *ablenken* |
| (to) disturb | *stören* |
| (to) divide | *teilen* |
| dole | *Arbeitslosengeld* |
| domestic | *inländisch, einheimisch* |
| (to) double | *verdoppeln* |
| doubt | *Zweifel, zweifeln* |
| downtown | *Innenstadt* |
| drain | *Abfluss, (Abwasser-) Kanal: (fig.) Abwanderung* |
| (to) draw | *(Schlussfolgerungen) ziehen* |
| (to) dream | *träumen* |
| driving licence | *Führerschein* |
| drop | *Fall, Sturz* |
| drug | *Droge* |
| (to) dry | *trocknen* |
| due to | *infolge von* |
| during | *während* |
| dust | *Staub* |
| duty | *Dienst, Pflicht* |
| (to) earn | *(Geld) verdienen* |
| economic | *wirtschaftlich* |
| economical | *sparsam, wirtschaftlich* |
| economy | *Wirtschaft* |
| edge | *Rand, Kante* |
| editor | *Redakteur* |

| | |
|---|---|
| education | Erziehung, Ausbildung |
| effect | Wirkung |
| effort | Anstrengung |
| election | Wahl |
| electricity | Elektrizität |
| elevator | Aufzug |
| (to) embarrass | in Verlegenheit (eine peinliche Lage) bringen |
| emergency | Notfall |
| emigrant | Auswanderer(in) |
| (to) emigrate | auswandern |
| emigration | Auswanderung |
| (to) employ | beschäftigen, anstellen |
| employer | Arbeitgeber |
| (to) enable | ermöglichen |
| (to) enclose | (einem Brief) beilegen |
| (to) encourage | ermutigen |
| enemy | Feind |
| engine | Motor, Maschine |
| engineer | Ingenieur |
| enquiry | Anfrage |
| (to) entertain | jmdn. unterhalten |
| entertainment | Unterhaltung |
| entire | ganz |
| entrance | Eingang |
| entry | Eintritt |
| environment | Umwelt |
| equal | gleich |
| equality | Gleichheit |
| equipment | Ausrüstung |
| equivalent | entsprechend |
| (to) escape | entfliehen |
| established | gegründet |
| ethnic | Volks- |
| even | sogar |
| event | Ereignis |
| evil | übel, böse |
| exact | genau |
| exam | Prüfung |
| (to) examine | untersuchen |
| excellent | ausgezeichnet |
| except | außer |
| exception | Ausnahme |
| (to) exchange | tauschen |
| (to) execute | ausführen; (ein Urteil) vollstrecken, hinrichten |
| (to) exercise | trainieren, üben |
| existence | Dasein, Leben |
| (to) expect | erwarten |

| | |
|---|---|
| expensive | *teuer* |
| experience | *Erfahrung* |
| experienced | *erfahren* |
| experiment | *Versuch* |
| (to) explain | *erklären* |
| explanation | *Erklärung* |
| (to) explode | *explodieren* |
| (to) explore | *erforschen* |
| (to) express | *ausdrücken* |
| extremely | *äußerst, außerordentlich* |
| (to) face | *sich gegenübersehen* |
| fact | *Tatsache* |
| factory | *Fabrik* |
| (to) fail | *(bei einer Prüfung) durchfallen* |
| failure | *Misserfolg* |
| fairly | *ziemlich* |
| false | *falsch* |
| familiar | *vertraut* |
| famous | *berühmt* |
| fare | *(Flug-) Kosten, Preis, Fahrpreis* |
| fashion | *Mode* |
| fast | *schnell* |
| fat | *fett* |
| fate | *Schicksal* |
| fault | *Fehler* |
| favour | *Gefälligkeit* |
| favourable | *günstig* |
| favourite | *Lieblings-* |
| fear | *Angst* |
| feature | *Merkmal, Eigenschaft; Reportage* |
| (to) be fed up | *sauer sein* |
| (to) feed | *ernähren, füttern* |
| (to) feel | *fühlen* |
| female | *weiblich* |
| fence | *Zaun* |
| ferry | *Fähre* |
| fever | *Fieber* |
| few | *wenig(e)* |
| fight | *Kampf* |
| final | *endgültig* |
| finally | *schließlich* |
| fine | *Geldstrafe* |
| (to) fire | *entlassen* |
| firm | *Firma* |
| first aid | *Erste Hilfe* |
| (to) fit | *passen (Anzug, Kleid)* |
| fixed | *fest* |
| flake | *Flocke* |

| | |
|---|---|
| flash | *Blitz, Blitzlicht* |
| flat | *flach* |
| flat | *Wohnung* |
| (to) flatter | *schmeicheln* |
| (to) flee | *fliehen* |
| flight | *Flug* |
| (to) float | *(an der Oberfläche) schwimmen* |
| (to) flood | *überfluten* |
| flour | *Mehl* |
| (to) flow | *fließen* |
| flow chart | *Flussdiagramm* |
| focus | *Mittelpunkt* |
| (to) fold | *falten* |
| (to) follow | *folgen* |
| food | *Essen, Nahrung* |
| for good | *endgültig* |
| (to) forbid | *verbieten* |
| force | *Gewalt* |
| (to) force | *zwingen* |
| forehead | *Stirn* |
| foreign | *ausländisch* |
| forest | *Wald* |
| forever | *für immer* |
| (to) forget | *vergessen* |
| fork | *Gabel* |
| (to) form | *bilden* |
| formal | *förmlich, formell* |
| fortune | *Vermögen* |
| forward | *nach vorn* |
| frame | *Rahmen* |
| (to) frame | *reinlegen* |
| freak | *Fanatiker(in)* |
| free of charge | *kostenlos* |
| freeway | *Autobahn* |
| (to) freeze | *(er)frieren, gefrieren, erstarren* |
| freight | *Güter, Fracht* |
| frequently | *oft, häufig* |
| fresh | *frisch* |
| fries | *Pommes frites* |
| frontier | *Grenzland, Grenze* |
| (to) frown | *die Stirn runzeln* |
| frustrated | *enttäuscht, unbefriedigt* |
| fuel | *Treibstoff* |
| fun | *Spaß* |
| funeral | *Begräbnis* |
| furniture | *Möbel* |
| furthest | *am weitesten* |
| gadget | *Gerät* |
| (to) gain | *gewinnen, profitieren* |

| | |
|---|---|
| game | *Spiel* |
| gap | *Lücke* |
| garlic | *Knoblauch* |
| gas | *Benzin* [AE], BE: *petrol* |
| (to) gasp | *keuchen* |
| gate | *Tor, Sperre; Flugsteig* |
| GCSE | *Abschluss der Sekundarstufe I* |
| gene | *Gen* |
| general | *allgemein* |
| generally | *im Allgemeinen* |
| generation | *Generation, Menschenalter* |
| (to) get rid of | *los werden* |
| (to) get up | *aufstehen* |
| (to) get used to | *sich gewöhnen an* |
| ghost | *Geist, Gespenst* |
| giant | *riesig* |
| gift | *Gabe, Begabung* |
| (to) give a hand | *behilflich sein* |
| (to) give up | *aufgeben, aufhören* |
| glad | *froh, erfreut, freudig* |
| glamour | *Glanz* |
| glasses | *Brille* |
| glider | *Segelflugzeug* |
| global | *weltweit* |
| glorious | *glorreich, prächtig* |
| glory | *Ruhm* |
| glove | *Handschuh* |
| GM (= genetically modified) food | *gentechnisch veränderte Nahrungsmittel* |
| goal | *Ziel, Tor* |
| good-bye | *Auf Wiedersehen, Lebewohl!* |
| goods | *Waren* |
| (to) govern | *regieren* |
| government | *Regierung* |
| (to) grab | *ergreifen, packen* |
| grade | *Rang, Note* |
| gradually | *allmählich* |
| grammar school | *Gymnasium* |
| (to) grant | *gewähren, bewilligen* |
| grape | *(Wein)traube* |
| grateful | *dankbar* |
| grave | *Grab* |
| great | *groß, großartig* |
| greeting | *Begrüßung, Gruß* |
| grey [AE], gray [BE] | *grau* |
| (to) grow | *wachsen* |
| growth | *Wachstum* |

| | |
|---|---|
| (to) guard | *bewachen* |
| (to) guess | *(er)raten, vermuten* |
| guest | *Gast* |
| gun | *(Schuss-) Waffe* |
| gun control | *Waffenkontrolle* |
| guy | *Typ, Bursche* |
| habit | *Gewohnheit, Angewohnheit* |
| (to) hack | *hacken, zerstückeln; in Computer eindringen* |
| hairdresser | *Friseur, Friseurin* |
| half | *halb; Hälfte* |
| hall | *Diele* |
| ham | *Schinken* |
| (to) handle | *handhaben, behandeln* |
| handsome | *gut aussehend, hübsch* |
| (to) happen | *sich ereignen* |
| harbour | *Hafen* |
| hardly | *kaum* |
| hardware | *Eisenwaren; Computerhardware* |
| hate | *Hass; hassen* |
| heading | *Überschrift* |
| headline | *Schlagzeile* |
| health | *Gesundheit* |
| healthy | *gesund* |
| heart | *Herz* |
| heat | *Hitze* |
| heavy | *schwer* |
| height | *Höhe* |
| helmet | *Helm* |
| help | *Hilfe* |
| hero | *Held* |
| (to) hesitate | *zögern, zaudern* |
| (to) hide | *verbergen* |
| highlight | *Höhepunkt* |
| (to) hire | *mieten* |
| history | *Geschichte* |
| hold | *Halt* |
| hole | *Loch* |
| honest | *ehrlich* |
| honour | *Ehre* |
| (to) hope | *hoffen* |
| hostel | *Heim, Herberge* |
| household | *Haushalt* |
| however | *jedoch* |
| (to) hug | *umarmen* |
| huge | *riesig* |
| human | *menschlich* |
| (to) hunt | *jagen* |

| | |
|---|---|
| (to) hurry | *sich beeilen* |
| (to) hurt | *verletzen* |
| husband | *(Ehe-) Mann* |
| idea | *Vorstellung* |
| ideal | *vorbildlich* |
| identity | *Identität* |
| illegal | *ungesetzlich, rechtswidrig* |
| (to) illustrate | *veranschaulichen* |
| (to) imagine | *sich vorstellen* |
| immediate | *unmittelbar, sofort* |
| immense | *ungeheuer, unermesslich* |
| immigrant | *Einwanderer* |
| (to) immigrate | *einwandern* |
| immigration | *Einwanderung* |
| imperfect | *fehlerhaft* |
| importance | *Wichtigkeit* |
| important | *wichtig* |
| impossible | *unmöglich* |
| (to) impress | *imponieren, beeindrucken* |
| impression | *Eindruck* |
| (to) improve | *sich verbessern, vorankommen* |
| improvement | *Verbesserung* |
| in favour of | *für* |
| in general | *im Allgemeinen* |
| in spite of | *trotz* |
| (to) include | *einschließen, enthalten, umfassen* |
| incorrect | *falsch, unrichtig* |
| (to) increase | *zunehmen, steigen* |
| increase | *Erhöhung, Zunahme, Steigerung* |
| increasing | *zunehmend, steigend* |
| indeed | *in der Tat, gewiss* |
| independent | *unabhängig* |
| indoor | *Innen-, drinnen* |
| industrial | *industriell* |
| influence | *Einfluss* |
| (to) inform | *benachrichtigen* |
| informal | *locker* |
| information | *Information* |
| initiative | *(Eigen)initiative* |
| injection | *Injektion* |
| (to) injure | *verletzen* |
| injury | *Verletzung* |
| inside | *drinnen* |
| instead | *statt dessen, anstatt* |
| instruction | *Anweisung, Gebrauchsanweisung* |
| insurance | *Versicherung* |

| | |
|---|---|
| intelligent | klug, intelligent |
| interest | Interesse; Zins |
| (to) interrupt | unterbrechen |
| interview | Vorstellungsgespräch |
| (to) introduce | (jmdn., sich) vorstellen |
| (to) invade | eindringen |
| (to) invent | erfinden |
| invention | Erfindung |
| (to) investigate | untersuchen |
| invitation | Einladung |
| (to) invite | einladen |
| involved | betroffen, beeinträchtigt |
| (to) iron | bügeln |
| iron | Eisen |
| irregular | ungleichmäßig, uneben |
| island | Insel |
| issue | Streitfrage |
| item | Artikel, Posten; Punkt |
| jam | Marmelade |
| jar | Glas (-gefäß) |
| jealous | eifersüchtig |
| Jew | Jude, Jüdin |
| jewellery | Schmuck |
| job | Stellung, Arbeitsstelle |
| (to) join | sich anschließen, beitreten, mitmachen |
| joke | Witz |
| journalist | Journalist |
| journey | Reise |
| judge | Richter |
| juice | Saft |
| (to) jump | springen |
| junk food | Nahrung ohne Nährwert |
| justice | Gerechtigkeit |
| (to) justify | rechtfertigen |
| keen on | scharf auf |
| (to) keep | (be-) halten |
| keyboard | Tastatur |
| (to) kick | treten |
| kid | Kind |
| kind | freundlich, liebenswürdig |
| kind | Art |
| kingdom | Königreich |
| kiss | Kuss |
| kitchen | Küche |
| kite | Drachen |
| knife | Messer |
| (to) knock | klopfen |

| | |
|---|---|
| knowledge | *Kenntnisse, Wissen* |
| label | *Etikett* |
| labour | *Arbeit* |
| labourer | *Arbeiter, Arbeitskraft* |
| ladder | *Leiter* |
| lake | *(Binnen-) See* |
| landscape | *Landschaft* |
| lane | *Fahrspur* |
| language | *Sprache* |
| (to) last | *dauern* |
| late | *spät* |
| lately | *kürzlich, in letzter Zeit* |
| latest | *neuesten* |
| laughter | *Gelächter* |
| laundry | *Schmutzwäsche* |
| lawyer | *Rechtsanwalt* |
| (to) lay | *legen; (den Tisch) decken* |
| (to) lead | *führen* |
| leaf | *Blatt* |
| league | *Liga* |
| (to) leave | *verlassen* |
| legend | *Legende* |
| (to) lend | *etwas verleihen* |
| length | *Länge* |
| less | *weniger* |
| lesson | *Unterrichtsstunde, Lektion* |
| lethal | *tödlich* |
| letter to the editor | *Leserbrief* |
| level | *Höhe, Niveau* |
| librarian | *Bibliothekar* |
| library | *Bücherei* |
| licence | *Genehmigung* |
| life story | *Biographie* |
| (to) lift | *heben* |
| light | *leicht* |
| likely | *wahrscheinlich* |
| (to) limit | *begrenzen* |
| link | *Verbindung* |
| (to) listen | *hören (Radio)* |
| lit | *angezündet* |
| live | *direkt (TV- oder Radiosendung)* |
| load | *Last* |
| local | *örtlich* |
| lock | *(Tür-) Schloss* |
| locker | *Schließfach* |
| (to) log in | *sich bei einem Computer anmelden* |
| lonely | *einsam, allein* |

| | |
|---|---|
| (to) look forward to | *sich freuen auf* |
| loose | *locker* |
| (to) lose | *verlieren* |
| loss | *Verlust* |
| low | *niedrig; leise (Stimme)* |
| lunch time | *Mittagspause* |
| lungs | *Lunge* |
| machine | *Maschine* |
| mad | *verrückt* |
| magazine | *Zeitschrift* |
| mail | *Post* |
| main | *Haupt-* |
| mainly | *hauptsächlich* |
| major | *größer, wichtiger* |
| majority | *Mehrheit* |
| (to) make a speech | *eine Rede halten* |
| management | *(Geschäfts-) Führung, Verwaltung* |
| manager | *Leiter, Direktor* |
| manners | *Manieren* |
| manual | *Handbuch* |
| manufacturer | *Hersteller* |
| marks | *(Schul-) Noten* |
| marriage | *Heirat, Ehe* |
| married | *verheiratet* |
| mass | *(kirchliche) Messe* |
| (to) match | *(farblich) passen* |
| mate | *Freund* |
| material | *Material* |
| maths | *Mathe* |
| maybe | *vielleicht* |
| maze | *Labyrinth* |
| meal | *Mahlzeit* |
| (to) mean | *bedeuten* |
| meaning | *Sinn, Bedeutung* |
| means | *Mittel* |
| measure | *Maß, Maßnahme* |
| (to) measure | *messen* |
| mechanic | *Mechaniker* |
| media | *die Medien* |
| (to) meet | *sich treffen* |
| meeting | *Treffen, Versammlung, Zusammenkunft* |
| (to) melt | *schmelzen* |
| member | *Mitglied* |
| memory | *Gedächtnis* |
| (to) mention | *erwähnen* |
| message | *Nachricht, Botschaft* |
| messenger | *Laufbursche, Bote, Bürobote* |

| | |
|---|---|
| middle | *Mitte* |
| mill | *Mühle, Fabrik, Werk* |
| mind | *Sinn, Verstand* |
| (to) mind | *ausmachen (in Sätzen wie: Es macht mir nichts aus …)* |
| mine | *Bergwerk* |
| miner | *Bergmann* |
| minimum wage | *Mindestlohn* |
| minority | *Minderheit* |
| minute | *Minute; winzig* |
| misfit | *Außenseiter* |
| (to) miss | *verpassen, vermissen* |
| (to) mix | *mischen* |
| mixture | *Mischung* |
| model | *Modell* |
| modest | *bescheiden* |
| moon | *Mond* |
| most | *die meisten* |
| motorbike | *Motorrad* |
| motorcyclist | *Motorradfahrer/in* |
| move | *Bewegung, Zug; sich bewegen, umziehen* |
| movement | *Bewegung* |
| (to) murder | *ermorden* |
| murder | *Mord* |
| murderer | *Mörder* |
| muscle | *Muskel* |
| musician | *Musiker* |
| mustn't | *darf nicht* |
| mysterious | *geheimnisvoll* |
| mystery | *Geheimnis, Rätsel* |
| narrow | *eng, schmal* |
| native | *(Ur-) Einwohner* |
| native | *angeboren, einheimisch* |
| near | *nahe, in der Nähe* |
| nearly | *fast, beinahe* |
| neat | *ordentlich, sauber* |
| need | *Bedürfnis, Bedarf; brauchen* |
| needn't | *braucht nicht, muss nicht* |
| neighbourhood | *Nachbarschaft* |
| neither | *keine (r, s)* |
| nephew | *Neffe* |
| nerve | *Nerv* |
| news | *Nachrichten (-sendung)* |
| newspaper | *Tageszeitung* |
| nickname | *Spitzname* |
| niece | *Nichte* |
| nil | *nichts* |

| | |
|---|---|
| noble | *edel, großzügig* |
| nobody | *niemand* |
| noise | *Lärm, Krach* |
| (to) nominate | *nominieren, aufstellen* |
| nor | *auch nicht* |
| nor do I | *ich auch nicht* |
| not yet | *noch nicht* |
| (to) note | *beachten* |
| notebook | *Notizbuch* |
| notes | *Notizen* |
| nought | *Null* |
| nowadays | *heutzutage* |
| nurse | *Krankenschwester, Krankenpfleger(in)* |
| oak | *Eiche* |
| (to) object | *Einspruch erheben* |
| occasion | *Anlass* |
| (to) offend | *beleidigen* |
| offer | *Angebot; anbieten* |
| office | *Büro* |
| opinion | *Meinung, Ansicht* |
| opportunity | *(günstige) Gelegenheit* |
| opposite | *gegenüber, entgegengesetzt; das Gegenteil* |
| opposition | *Widerstand* |
| option | *Wahl* |
| order | *Auftrag* |
| ordinary | *gewöhnlich* |
| (to) organize | *organisieren* |
| origin | *Ursprung* |
| otherwise | *sonst* |
| ought | *sollte (eigentlich)* |
| out of work | *arbeitslos* |
| outdoor | *im Freien* |
| outline | *Umriss* |
| (to) overcome | *überwinden* |
| overseas | *Auslands-, ausländisch* |
| (to) owe | *schulden* |
| owing to | *dank* |
| (to) own | *besitzen* |
| owner | *Besitzer* |
| pack | *Bündel* |
| padding | *Polsterung* |
| pain | *Schmerz* |
| painful | *schmerzhaft* |
| pale | *bleich* |
| panic | *Panik* |
| paramedic | *ärztlicher Assistent/ärztliche Assistentin* |
| pardon | *wie bitte?* |

| | |
|---|---|
| park | *(Auto) parken* |
| particular | *bestimmt, besonder-* |
| particularly | *besonders* |
| party | *Partei* |
| (to) pass | *vorbeigehen (an)* |
| passenger | *Reisender, Fahrgast, Passagier* |
| password | *Parole, Passwort* |
| past | *vorüber, vorbei* |
| patient | *geduldig* |
| pay | *Bezahlung; bezahlen* |
| payment | *Zahlung, Bezahlung* |
| penalty | *Strafe* |
| pencil | *Bleistift* |
| perfect | *vollkommen* |
| performance | *(Film-, Theater-) Vorstellung; Leistung* |
| period | *Zeitspanne* |
| permission | *Erlaubnis* |
| persecution | *Verfolgung* |
| (to) persuade | *überzeugen, überreden* |
| pet | *Haustier* |
| petrol | *Benzin* |
| physical | *körperlich* |
| physical science | *Naturwissenschaft* |
| physics | *Physik* |
| (to) pick | *(Früchte) pflücken; etwas abholen, aufheben* |
| piece | *Stück* |
| pigeon | *Taube* |
| pilgrim | *Pilger* |
| pill | *Tablette* |
| pilot | *Pilot* |
| pin | *Stecknadel* |
| pity | *Mitleid* |
| plane | *Flugzeug; Fläche, Ebene* |
| planet | *Planet* |
| plant | *Fabrikanlage, Werk* |
| plate | *Teller* |
| platform | *(Wahl-) Programm* |
| pleasant | *angenehm* |
| pleased | *zufrieden* |
| pleasure | *Vergnügen* |
| plug | *Stecker* |
| poem | *Gedicht* |
| poetry | *Dichtung* |
| point | *Spitze* |
| poison | *Gift* |
| police | *Polizei* |

| | |
|---|---|
| (to) polish | *polieren* |
| polite | *höflich* |
| political | *politisch* |
| politician | *Politiker* |
| politics | *Politik* |
| (to) pollute | *verschmutzen* |
| pollution | *(Umwelt-) Verschmutzung* |
| popular | *beliebt* |
| population | *Bevölkerung* |
| position | *Stellung, Lage* |
| (to) possess | *besitzen* |
| possession | *Besitz* |
| possibility | *Möglichkeit* |
| possible | *möglich* |
| (to) post | *auf die Post geben* |
| pot | *Kanne, Topf* |
| potato | *Kartoffel* |
| (to) pour | *gießen* |
| poverty | *Armut* |
| power | *Kraft, Stärke* |
| (to) practise | *üben* |
| (to) prefer | *(etwas) vorziehen* |
| (to) present | *überreichen, schenken* |
| present | *gegenwärtig, momentan* |
| presenter | *Moderator* |
| (to) press | *bügeln* |
| pressure | *(nervlicher) Druck* |
| pretty | *hübsch; ziemlich* |
| previous | *vorhergehend* |
| price | *(Bezahl-) Preis* |
| pride | *Stolz* |
| primary school | *Grundschule* |
| prime minister | *Premierminister* |
| (to) print | *drucken* |
| prison | *Gefängnis* |
| prize | *Preis (= Gewinn), Auszeichnung* |
| (to) process | *verarbeiten, bearbeiten* |
| (to) produce | *herstellen* |
| profit | *Gewinn* |
| progress | *Fortschritt* |
| promise | *Versprechen; versprechen* |
| (to) pronounce | *aussprechen* |
| proof | *Beweis* |
| proper | *passend, richtig, geeignet* |
| properly | *anständig, ange-messen* |

| | |
|---|---|
| **property** | *Eigentum, Grundstück* |
| **(to) protect** | *(be)schützen* |
| **protective** | *Schutz-, schützend* |
| **proud** | *stolz* |
| **(to) prove** | *beweisen* |
| **(to) provide** | *sorgen (für), versorgen* |
| **public** | *öffentlich* |
| **public facilities** | *öffentliche Einrichtungen* |
| **public transport** | *öffentliche Verkehrsmittel* |
| **(to) pull down** | *(ein Haus) abreißen* |
| **(to) punish** | *bestrafen* |
| **punishment** | *Strafe* |
| **pupil** | *Schüler/in* |
| **puzzle** | *(Kreuzwort-) Rätsel* |
| **qualified** | *ausgebildet, qualifiziert* |
| **queue** | *Schlange* |
| **quite** | *ganz, ziemlich* |
| **quote** | *Zitat; zitieren* |
| **race** | *Rasse* |
| **racial** | *rassisch, Rassen-* |
| **racism** | *Rassismus* |
| **racist** | *Rassist* |
| **rail** | *Bahn, Gleis* |
| **railway** | *Eisenbahn* |
| **(to) raise** | *(Frage) aufwerfen; (Stimme, Hand) erheben* |
| **range** | *Auswahl* |
| **rank** | *Rang* |
| **rare** | *selten* |
| **rate** | *Quote, Anteil; Verhältnis* |
| **rather** | *lieber* |
| **(to) rattle** | *klappern* |
| **(to) react** | *reagieren* |
| **reality** | *Wirklichkeit* |
| **reason** | *Grund, Anlass* |
| **reasonable** | *vernünftig, angemessen* |
| **(to) receive** | *erhalten, bekommen* |
| **recent** | *jüngst, neu* |
| **recess** | *Pause* |
| **(to) recommend** | *empfehlen* |
| **(to) record** | *aufzeichnen* |
| **(to) recover** | *wiedererlangen; sich erholen* |
| **(to) recycle** | *wieder aufbereiten* |
| **(to) reduce** | *herabsetzen, verringern* |

| | |
|---|---|
| (to) refer | *sich beziehen (auf)* |
| (to) refuse | *abschlagen, sich weigern* |
| (to) regret | *bedauern* |
| regular | *regelmäßig* |
| rehearsal | *Probe* |
| relative | *Verwandte(r)* |
| (to) relax | *sich entspannen* |
| release | *Freilassung* |
| (to) remain | *bleiben* |
| (to) remember | *daran denken, sich erinnern* |
| (to) remind | *erinnern (an)* |
| remote control | *Fernbedienung* |
| (to) remove | *beseitigen, entfernen* |
| rent | *Miete* |
| (to) repeat | *wiederholen* |
| (to) replace | *ersetzen* |
| reply | *Antwort; antworten* |
| report | *Bericht; berichten* |
| representative | *Vertreter* |
| reputation | *Ruf* |
| request | *Bitte, Wunsch* |
| (to) rescue | *retten* |
| research | *Forschung* |
| resident | *Bewohner, Einwohner* |
| (to) resign | *zurücktreten* |
| respect | *Hinsicht* |
| responsibility | *Verantwortung* |
| responsible | *verantwortlich* |
| retraining | *Umschulung* |
| (to) return | *zurückkehren* |
| review | *Kritik* |
| revision | *Wiederholung* |
| revolution | *Revolution, Umsturz* |
| rhyme | *Reim* |
| rhythm | *Rhythmus* |
| rice | *Reis* |
| (to) ride | *(Motorrad, Fahrrad) fahren* |
| rig | *Ölbohrinsel* |
| riot | *(Straßen-) Schlacht, Krawall* |
| (to) rise | *ansteigen* |
| rival | *Konkurrent* |
| river | *Fluss* |
| road | *Straße* |
| (to) rob | *be-, ausrauben* |
| robot | *Roboter* |
| rock | *Stein* |
| rocket | *Rakete* |
| role | *Rolle* |

| | |
|---|---|
| roof | *Dach* |
| rope | *Seil, Tau* |
| rough | *rau, grob* |
| round | *rund* |
| route | *Route, Strecke* |
| rubber | *Gummi* |
| rubbish | *Abfall, Müll* |
| rucksack | *Rucksack* |
| rude | *unhöflich* |
| rule | *Bestimmung, Verbot, Vorschrift* |
| rumour | *Gerücht* |
| runway | *Startbahn* |
| safe | *sicher* |
| safety | *Sicherheit* |
| salary | *(Geld) Gehalt* |
| sales | *Umsatz, Verkäufe* |
| (to) satisfy | *zufrieden stellen* |
| sausage | *Wurst* |
| (to) save | *retten; aufbewahren* |
| (to) saw | *sägen* |
| (to) scan | *abtasten, scannen* |
| scared | *verängstigt* |
| scarf | *Schal* |
| scary | *Furcht erregend* |
| schedule | *Zeit-/Fahrplan* |
| scheme | *Plan, Konzept, Projekt* |
| scholarship | *Stipendium* |
| school leaver | *Schulabgänger* |
| science | *(Natur-) Wissenschaft* |
| science fiction | *Zukunftsroman* |
| scissors | *Schere* |
| screen | *Bildschirm, (Film-) Leinwand* |
| script | *Drehbuch* |
| search | *Nachforschung, Suche* |
| seaside | *Küste* |
| season | *Jahreszeit* |
| seat | *Sitz, Sitzplatz* |
| seat belt | *Sicherheitsgurt* |
| secondary school | *höhere (weiterführende) Schule* |
| secret | *Geheimnis* |
| secretary | *Sekretär/in* |
| section | *Teil* |
| seed | *Saat, Same* |
| seldom | *selten* |
| (to) sell | *verkaufen* |
| (to) send | *zuschicken* |
| senior | *älter* |
| sense | *Sinn, Verstand* |
| sensible | *vernünftig* |

| | |
|---|---|
| sentence | *Urteil(sspruch)* |
| (to) sentence | *verurteilen* |
| (to) separate [eit] | *trennen, (ab)teilen* |
| separate [it] | *getrennt, abgesondert* |
| series | *Reihe* |
| serious | *ernst, ernsthaft* |
| servant | *Diener* |
| (to) serve | *bedienen* |
| service | *Bedienung; Dienst* |
| set | *(Fernseh-) Apparat* |
| (to) settle | *sich niederlassen; besiedeln* |
| settlement | *Siedlung, Niederlassung* |
| several | *einige, mehrere* |
| shadow | *Schatten* |
| shame | *Schande; Schamgefühl* |
| shape | *Umriss, Gestalt, Form* |
| share | *Aktie, Anteil* |
| (to) share | *sich teilen* |
| sharp | *scharf* |
| shawl | *Schultertuch* |
| (to) shelter | *sich schützen, Schutz suchen* |
| shelter | *Schutz* |
| shift (work) | *Schicht (-arbeit)* |
| ship | *Schiff* |
| shirt | *Hemd* |
| shock | *Schock* |
| shoplifter | *Ladendieb* |
| shore | *Küste, Ufer* |
| shot | *Schuss* |
| (to) shout | *schreien* |
| shower | *Dusche* |
| (to) shut | *schließen* |
| shut | *geschlossen* |
| shy | *schüchtern* |
| sidewalk | *Bürgersteig, Gehweg* |
| sigh | *Seufzer* |
| sight | *Anblick* |
| sights | *Sehenswürdigkeiten* |
| silence | *Stille* |
| silly | *albern, dumm* |
| similar | *ähnlich* |
| simulation | *Imitation, Nachahmung* |
| sincere | *aufrichtig* |
| single | *einzeln; ledig* |
| siren | *Sirene* |
| sister | *Schwester* |
| situation | *Situation* |

| | |
|---|---|
| size | *Größe* |
| skilful | *geschickt, gewandt* |
| skill | *Fähigkeit* |
| skilled | *gelernt* |
| skin | *Haut* |
| skirt | *Rock* |
| slave | *Sklave* |
| sled | *Schlitten* |
| (to) slide | *gleiten, rutschen* |
| slight | *schwach, klein, unbedeutend* |
| slogan | *Werbespruch* |
| slope | *Hang* |
| slow motion | *Zeitlupe* |
| (to) smash | *zerschmettern, zerschlagen* |
| smell | *Geruch* |
| (to) smile | *lächeln* |
| (to) smoke | *rauchen* |
| snake | *Schlange* |
| snooker | *Billard* |
| snow | *Schnee* |
| soap | *Seife* |
| soccer | *(europäischer) Fußball* |
| social | *gesellschaftlich* |
| society | *Gesellschaft* |
| soil | *Erdboden* |
| solar | *Solar-, Sonnen-* |
| solution | *Lösung* |
| (to) solve | *lösen, auflösen* |
| son | *Sohn* |
| songwriter | *Liedermacher* |
| sore | *wund* |
| (to) sound | *klingen, tönen* |
| soup | *Suppe* |
| source | *Quelle* |
| space | *Raum* |
| spare time | *Freizeit* |
| spark | *Funke* |
| (to) speculate | *vermuten* |
| speech | *Rede* |
| (to) spell | *buchstabieren* |
| (to) spend | *(Geld) ausgeben* |
| (to) spoil | *verderben, verschandeln* |
| (to) spray | *besprühen, bespritzen* |
| (to) spread | *ausbreiten, verteilen* |
| spring | *Frühling* |
| square | *öffentlicher Platz, Viereck* |
| staff | *Personal* |

| | |
|---|---|
| stage | *Stadium, Phase* |
| stain | *Fleck* |
| stairs | *Stufen, Treppe* |
| stamp | *Stempel; Briefmarke* |
| standard of living | *Lebensstandard* |
| (to) state | *feststellen, mitteilen* |
| statement | *Darstellung; Behauptung* |
| statistics | *Statistik* |
| (to) stay | *bleiben* |
| steady | *stetig; fest; standhaft* |
| steam | *Dampf* |
| steam engine | *Dampfmaschine* |
| step | *Schritt; Stufe* |
| stiff | *steif* |
| still | *noch* |
| stomach | *Magen* |
| store | *Laden, Geschäft* |
| straight | *gerade, direkt* |
| strength | *Kraft, Stärke* |
| (to) stretch | *sich erstrecken* |
| strict | *streng* |
| strike | *Streik* |
| string | *Schnur* |
| struggle | *Kampf; kämpfen* |
| study | *Studie* |
| stuff | *Zeug* |
| stupid | *dumm* |
| style | *Stil* |
| subject | *Thema, Gegenstand* |
| suburb | *Vorort, Stadtrandsiedlung* |
| subway | *Unterführung, U-Bahn* |
| (to) succeed in | *erfolgreich sein* |
| success | *Erfolg* |
| suddenly | *plötzlich* |
| (to) suffer | *leiden (an)* |
| suffix | *Nachsilbe* |
| (to) suggest | *vorschlagen* |
| suggestion | *Anregung, Vorschlag* |
| (to) suit | *passen* |
| supply | *Angebot, Vorrat; liefern* |
| (to) support | *unterstützen* |
| supporter | *Anhänger* |
| (to) suppose | *annehmen, vermuten* |
| sure | *sicher, gewiss* |
| surface | *Oberfläche* |
| surprise | *Überraschung* |
| survey | *Untersuchung, Studie* |

| | |
|---|---|
| (to) survive | *überleben* |
| (to) suspect | *argwöhnen, vermuten* |
| (to) swear | *schwören* |
| (to) sweat | *schwitzen* |
| (to) sweep | *fegen, kehren* |
| system | *System* |
| (to) take part in | *teilnehmen an* |
| take-off | *Start (eines Flugzeugs)* |
| talent | *Begabung* |
| talk | *Gespräch* |
| tape | *Tonband* |
| task | *Aufgabe* |
| (to) taste | *schmecken* |
| tax | *Steuer* |
| (to) teach | *unterrichten* |
| team | *Mannschaft* |
| (to) tear | *zerreißen, zerren; abreißen* |
| technical | *technisch* |
| technology | *Technologie* |
| teeth | *Zähne* |
| temper | *Stimmung* |
| temperature | *Temperatur* |
| tendency | *Tendenz, Neigung* |
| tent | *Zelt* |
| term | *Bedingung; Trimester* |
| terrible | *schrecklich* |
| than | *als (nach Komparativ)* |
| Thanksgiving | *amerikanisches Erntedankfest* |
| theory | *Theorie* |
| (to) think | *denken* |
| thirst | *Durst* |
| thirsty | *durstig* |
| thought | *Gedanke* |
| thoughtful | *nachdenklich* |
| (to) threaten | *bedrohen* |
| thriller | *Reißer, Krimi* |
| throat | *Hals, Kehle* |
| (to) throw | *werfen* |
| (to) tie | *binden* |
| tight | *eng; dicht* |
| timetable | *Fahrplan* |
| tin | *Zinn; Dose, Büchse* |
| tip | *Trinkgeld* |
| toe | *Zehe* |
| together | *zusammen* |
| tongue | *Zunge* |
| tonight | *heute Abend* |
| tool | *Werkzeug* |
| (to) touch | *berühren* |

| | |
|---|---|
| tough | *zäh* |
| tourist | *Tourist* |
| towel | *Handtuch* |
| toy | *Spielzeug* |
| track | *(Fuß-) Spur* |
| trade | *Handel; Beruf* |
| trade union | *Gewerkschaft* |
| traffic | *Verkehr* |
| traffic jam | *(Verkehrs-) Stau* |
| trainee | *Praktikant* |
| training | *Ausbildung* |
| transparency | *Folie, Transparentkopie* |
| transport | *Verkehrsmittel* |
| (to) travel | *reisen* |
| treasure | *Schatz* |
| (to) treat | *behandeln* |
| treatment | *Behandlung* |
| trial | *Prozess; Probe; Verhandlung* |
| tribe | *(Volks-) Stamm* |
| trouble | *Problem, Schwierigkeit* |
| trousers | *Hose* |
| (to) trust | *vertrauen* |
| tube | *Londons U-Bahn; Röhre* |
| tune | *Lied, Melodie* |
| twice | *zweimal* |
| (to) twist | *drehen* |
| (to) type | *Schreibmaschine schreiben* |
| typical (of) | *typisch (für)* |
| ugly | *hässlich* |
| umbrella | *Regenschirm* |
| unable | *unfähig, nicht in der Lage* |
| unbelievable | *unglaublich* |
| uncomfortable | *unbequem* |
| unemployed | *arbeitslos* |
| unemployment | *Arbeitslosigkeit* |
| unfriendly | *unfreundlich* |
| unhealthy | *ungesund* |
| unit | *Lektion* |
| (to) unite | *sich vereinigen* |
| unknown | *unbekannt, nicht bekannt* |
| unless | *wenn nicht* |
| (to) unload | *entladen* |
| unnecessary | *unnötig* |
| (to) unpack | *auspacken* |
| unpopular | *unbeliebt* |
| unskilled | *ungelernt* |

| | |
|---|---|
| unskilled worker | *Hilfsarbeiter* |
| untidy | *unordentlich* |
| unusual | *ungewöhnlich* |
| unwanted | *unerwünscht, störend* |
| upset | *aufgebracht, aufgeregt* |
| upside-down | *verkehrt herum, auf dem Kopf* |
| urgent | *dringend* |
| (to) use | *gebrauchen, nutzen* |
| useful | *nützlich* |
| useless | *nutzlos* |
| user-friendly | *benutzerfreundlich* |
| usual | *gewöhnlich* |
| vacation | *Ferien* |
| valley | *Tal* |
| valuable | *wertvoll* |
| value | *Wert* |
| van | *Transporter* |
| vandalism | *Zerstörungswut* |
| variety | *Auswahl, Mannigfaltigkeit* |
| vegetable | *Gemüse* |
| vegetarian | *Vegetarier* |
| vehicle | *Fahrzeug* |
| victim | *Opfer* |
| victory | *Sieg* |
| view | *Ansicht, Meinung; Aussicht* |
| vinegar | *Essig* |
| violence | *Gewalt, Gewalttätigkeit* |
| violent | *gewalttätig; heftig* |
| virtual | *so gut wie; nicht wirklich vorhanden* |
| vision | *Sehvermögen; Vorstellung* |
| (to) visit | *besuchen* |
| visitor | *Besucher* |
| vocabulary | *Wortschatz* |
| voice | *Stimme* |
| volleyball | *Volleyball* |
| volunteer | *Freiwilliger* |
| (to) vote | *abstimmen; wählen* |
| voyage | *Schiffsreise* |
| wage | *Lohn* |
| wallet | *Brieftasche* |
| war | *Krieg* |
| wardrobe | *(Kleider-) Schrank* |
| waste | *Abfall, Vergeudung, Verlust; verschwenden* |
| waste water | *Abwasser* |
| (to) watch | *sehen, fernsehen* |

| | |
|---|---|
| wave | Welle |
| wax | Wachs |
| weak | schwach |
| wealth | Wohlstand |
| wealthy | wohlhabend, reich |
| weapon | Waffe |
| (to) wear | (Kleid, Uniform) tragen |
| weather | Wetter |
| weekday | Wochentag |
| weekend | Wochenende |
| (to) weigh | wiegen |
| weight | Gewicht |
| weird | merkwürdig, seltsam |
| welcome | willkommen |
| welfare | Sozialhilfe |
| wet | nass |
| whale | Wal |
| whether | ob |
| while | während |
| (to) whisper | flüstern |
| whistle | Pfeife; Pfiff |
| whole | ganz |
| wholly | gänzlich |
| wide | breit |
| wife | Ehefrau |
| wing | Flügel |
| (to) wipe | (ab-) wischen, (ab-) trocknen |
| wire | Draht |
| wise | weise, Klug |
| within | drin, im Innern, innerhalb |
| without | ohne |
| witness | Zeuge |
| (to) wonder | sich fragen, sich wundern über |
| wood | Holz |
| working hours | Arbeitszeit, Arbeitsstunden |
| workshop | Arbeitsgemeinschaft |
| (to) worry about | sich Sorgen machen über |
| worse | schlechter, schlimmer |
| worth | wert (sein) |
| wound | Wunde |
| wrong | Unrecht; falsch, unrecht |
| (to) yawn | gähnen |
| young | jung |
| youth | Jugendlicher; Jugend |
| zero | Null |
| zoo | Tierpark, Zoo |

# Countries – People – Languages

| Country | Inhabitant | Language |
|---|---|---|
| Australia | Australian | English |
| Austria | Austrian | German |
| Belgium | Belgian | Flemish / French |
| Brazil | Brazilian | Portuguese |
| Britain | Briton | English |
| Canada | Canadian | English / French |
| Denmark | Dane | Danish |
| England | Englishman | English |
| Finland | Fin | Finnish / Swedish |
| France | Frenchman | French |
| Germany | German | German |
| Greece | Greek | Greek |
| Holland/Netherlands | Dutchman | Dutch |
| Hungary | Hungarian | Hungarian |
| India | Indian | Hindi / English |
| Ireland | Irishman | English / Gaelic |
| Italy | Italian | Italian |
| Japan | Japanese | Japanese |
| Mexico | Mexican | Spanish |
| New Zealand | New Zealander | English |
| Norway | Norwegian | Norwegian |
| Poland | Pole | Polish |

| Country | Inhabitant | Language |
|---|---|---|
| Portugal | Portuguese | Portuguese |
| Russia | Russian | Russian |
| Scotland | Scotsman | English / Gaelic |
| South Africa | South African | English / Afrikaans |
| Spain | Spaniard | Spanish |
| Sweden | Swede | Swedish |
| Switzerland | Swiss | German / French / Italian |
| Turkey | Turk | Turkish |
| United Kingdom | Briton | English |
| USA | American | English |
| Wales | Welshman | English / Gaelic |

# Britisches und amerikanisches Englisch

| deutsche Bedeutung | British English [BE] | American English [AE] |
|---|---|---|
| *Herbst* | autumn | fall |
| *Rechnung* | bill | check |
| *Keks* | biscuit | cookie |
| *Talkshow* | chat show | talk show |
| *Apotheke* | chemist's | pharmacy, drugstore |
| *Pommes frites* | chips [Pl.] | (French) fries [Pl.] |
| *Kino* | cinema | movie theater |
| *City, Innenstadt* | city centre | downtown |
| *Chips* | crisps [Pl.] | potato chips [Pl.] |
| *Führerschein* | driving licence | driver's license |
| *(Kino) Film* | film | movie |
| *1. Stock* | first floor | second floor |
| *Wohnung* | flat | apartment |
| *Fußball* | football | soccer |
| *Punkt* | full stop | period, bei Internetadressen: dot |
| *Erdgeschoss* | ground floor | first floor |
| *Handtasche* | handbag | purse, pocketbook |
| *ein Auto mieten* | (to) hire a car | (to) rent a car |
| *Urlaub* | holiday | vacation |
| *Schulferien,* | holidays [Pl.] | vacation |
| *Marmelade* | jam | jelly |

| deutsche Bedeutung | British English [BE] | American English [AE] |
|---|---|---|
| *Aufzug* | lift | elevator |
| *Autobahn* | motorway | highway, freeway |
| *Geldschein* | note | bill |
| *natürlich* | of course | sure |
| *Wie bitte?* | pardon?, sorry? | excuse me? |
| *Bürgersteig* | pavement | sidewalk |
| *Benzin* | petrol | gas, gasoline |
| *Tankstelle* | petrol station | gas station |
| *Briefkasten* | post-box | mailbox |
| *Postleitzahl* | postcode | zip code |
| *Portemonnaie* | purse | wallet, coin purse |
| *Warteschlange* | queue | line |
| *Gleis(e)* | rails [Pl.] | tracks [Pl.] |
| *Bahn* | railway | railroad |
| *Geschäft* | shop | store |
| *Entschuldigung!* | sorry | excuse me |
| *Fußgängerunterführung* | subway | (pedestrian) underpass |
| *Bonbon* | sweet | candy |
| *Taxi* | taxi | cab |
| *Fahrplan* | timetable | schedule |
| *W.C.* | toilet | bathroom, restroom |
| *Taschenlampe* | torch | flashlight |
| *Hose* | trousers [Pl.] | pants [Pl.] |
| *U-Bahn* | underground | subway |

# Unregelmäßige Verben

| Infinitive | Past Tense | Past Participle | deutsche Übersetzung |
|---|---|---|---|
| be | was | been | *sein* |
| bear | bore | born(e) | *(er)tragen; gebären* |
| beat | beat | beaten | *schlagen* |
| begin | began | begun | *beginnen* |
| bind | bound | bound | *binden* |
| bite | bit | bit(ten) | *beißen* |
| blow | blew | blown | *blasen* |
| break | broke | broken | *brechen* |
| bring | brought | brought | *bringen* |
| build | built | built | *bauen* |
| burn | burnt/ed | burnt/ed | *brennen* |
| buy | bought | bought | *kaufen* |
| catch | caught | caught | *fangen* |
| choose | chose | chosen | *wählen* |
| come | came | come | *kommen* |
| deal | dealt | dealt | *handeln* |
| do | did | done | *tun* |
| draw | drew | drawn | *zeichnen, ziehen* |
| dream | dreamt/ed | dreamt/ed | *träumen* |
| drink | drank | drunk | *trinken* |
| drive | drove | driven | *fahren* |
| eat | ate | eaten | *essen* |

| Infinitive | Past Tense | Past Participle | deutsche Übersetzung |
|---|---|---|---|
| fall | fell | fallen | *fallen* |
| feed | fed | fed | *füttern* |
| feel | felt | felt | *fühlen* |
| fight | fought | fought | *kämpfen* |
| find | found | found | *finden* |
| fly | flew | flown | *fliegen* |
| forbid | forbade | forbidden | *verbieten* |
| forget | forgot | forgotten | *vergessen* |
| forgive | forgave | forgiven | *vergeben* |
| freeze | froze | frozen | *frieren* |
| give | gave | given | *geben* |
| go | went | gone | *gehen* |
| grow | grew | grown | *wachsen* |
| hear | heard | heard | *hören* |
| hide | hid | hidden | *verstecken* |
| hold | held | held | *halten* |
| keep | kept | kept | *halten* |
| know | knew | known | *wissen* |
| lay | laid | laid | *legen* |
| lead | led | led | *leiten* |
| learn | learnt/ed | learnt/ed | *lernen* |
| leave | left | left | *lassen* |
| lend | lent | lent | *leihen* |
| lean | leant/ed | leant/ed | *lehnen* |
| lie | lay | lain | *liegen* |

| Infinitive | Past Tense | Past Participle | deutsche Übersetzung |
|---|---|---|---|
| lose | lost | lost | *verlieren* |
| make | made | made | *machen* |
| mean | meant | meant | *meinen, bedeuten* |
| meet | met | met | *treffen* |
| pay | paid | paid | *bezahlen* |
| read [iː] | read [e] | read [e] | *lesen* |
| ride | rode | ridden | *fahren, reiten* |
| ring | rang | rung | *läuten* |
| rise | rose | risen | *aufstehen, aufgehen* |
| run | ran | run | *laufen, rennen* |
| say | said | said | *sagen* |
| see | saw | seen | *sehen* |
| seek | sought | sought | *suchen* |
| sell | sold | sold | *verkaufen* |
| send | sent | sent | *senden* |
| shake | shook | shaken | *schütteln* |
| shine | shone | shone | *scheinen* |
| shoot | shot | shot | *schießen* |
| show | showed | shown | *zeigen* |
| shrink | shrank | shrunk | *schrumpfen, einlaufen* |
| sing | sang | sung | *singen* |
| sink | sank | sunk | *sinken* |
| sit | sat | sat | *sitzen* |
| sleep | slept | slept | *schlafen* |
| smell | smelt | smelt | *riechen* |

| Infinitive | Past Tense | Past Participle | deutsche Übersetzung |
|---|---|---|---|
| speak | spoke | spoken | *sprechen* |
| spell | spelt | spelt | *buchstabieren* |
| spend | spent | spent | *verbringen, ausgeben* |
| spring | sprang | sprung | *springen* |
| stand | stood | stood | *stehen* |
| steal | stole | stolen | *stehlen* |
| stick | stuck | stuck | *kleben* |
| swear | swore | sworn | *fluchen; schwören* |
| sweep | swept | swept | *fegen* |
| swim | swam | swum | *schwimmen* |
| swing | swung | swung | *schwingen* |
| take | took | taken | *nehmen* |
| teach | taught | taught | *lehren* |
| tear | tore | torn | *reißen* |
| tell | told | told | *erzählen* |
| think | thought | thought | *denken, glauben* |
| throw | threw | thrown | *werfen* |
| understand | understood | understood | *verstehen* |
| wake | woke | woken | *aufwachen, wecken* |
| wear | wore | worn | *tragen* |
| win | won | won | *gewinnen* |
| write | wrote | written | *schreiben* |

Notizen

Notizen

# Ihre Meinung ist uns wichtig!

Ihre Anregungen sind uns immer willkommen. Bitte informieren Sie uns mit diesem Schein über Ihre Verbesserungsvorschläge!

| Titel-Nr. | Seite | Vorschlag |
| --- | --- | --- |
| | | |
| | | |
| | | |
| | | |
| | | |
| | | |
| | | |
| | | |
| | | |
| | | |

Bitte hier abtrennen

*Die echten Hilfen zum Lernen …* **STARK**

Bitte hier abtrennen

## Zutreffendes bitte ankreuzen! Die Absenderin/der Absender ist:

- [ ] Lehrer/in den Klassenstufen: ______
- [ ] Fachbetreuer/in
  Fächer: ______
- [ ] Seminarlehrer/in
  Fächer: ______
- [ ] Regierungsfachberater/in
  Fächer: ______
- [ ] Oberstufenbetreuer/in
- [ ] Schulleiter/in
- [ ] Leiter/in Lehrerbibliothek
- [ ] Leiter/in Schülerbibliothek
- [ ] Referendar/in, Termin 2. Staatsexamen: ______
- [ ] Sekretariat
- [ ] Schüler/in, Klasse: ______
- [ ] Elternteil
- [ ] Sonstiges: ______

**STARK Verlag**
**Postfach 1852**
**85318 Freising**

17-V2X

Bitte ausfüllen und im frankierten Umschlag an uns einsenden. Für Fensterkuverts geeignet.

**Kennen Sie Ihre Kundennummer? Bitte hier eintragen.**

| | | | | | | |
|---|---|---|---|---|---|---|
| | | | | | | |

## Absender (Bitte in Druckbuchstaben!)

Name/Vorname

Straße/Nr.

PLZ/Ort

Telefon privat — Geburtsjahr

E-Mail

## Schule/Schulstempel (Bitte angeben!)

## Unterrichtsfächer: (Bei Lehrkräften!)

*(Bitte blättern Sie um)*